America
and
The Vatican

Trading Information
After World War II

Robert F. Illing

History Publishing Company
Palisades, New York

2011

Published in the United States by
History Publishing Company
Palisades, New York
www.historypublishingco.com

ISBN-10: 1-933909-69-2
ISBN-13: 978-1-933909-69-1
LCCN: 2010943090
SAN: 850-5942

Illing, Robert F.
     America and the Vatican : trading information after
World War II / Robert F. Illing.
     p. cm.
     Includes index.
     LCCN 2010940082
     ISBN-13: 978-1-933909-69-1
     ISBN-10: 1-933909-69-2

     1. Diplomatic and consular service, American--Vatican
City. 2. Catholic Church--Foreign relations--United
States. 3. United States--Foreign relations--Catholic
Church. 4. Illing, Robert F. 5. Diplomats--United
States--Biography.   I. Title.

JZ1480.A57V38 2011   327.730456'34
                           QBI11-200007

Printed in the United States on acid-free paper

9 8 7 6 5 4 3 2 1

First Edition

TO GEORGINA AND ARI

Contents

Acknowledgements

My editor, Alexis Starke, deserves my gratitude for her well-considered suggestions and observations on the draft, and Robert Aulicino for the exceptionally attractive cover design that reflects dramatically the themes of the book. Thanks to Angela Werner for her tasteful and well-crafted interior design, and Kendra Millis for the careful indexing of the contents, a job that required special care due to the numerous foreign names and words. I wish, too, to thank my publisher, Don Bracken, for his judgement in publishing my book. May Clio, the muse of history, and Pluto, the god of wealth, reward him justly for his judgment.

And a special thanks to my assistant Monica Coelho, who moved the entire process along smoothly with her knowledge of what to me were often the arcana of my laptop computer, and our housekeeper, Laurinda Coelho, who kept me well and happily nourished throughout with her delicious Portuguese cuisine. And, especially, I want to thank my wife Georgina, without whose encouragement and support this book would never have been written.

Henry Cabot Lodge and Robert Illing at the North American College, July 1970

Foreword

This book comes out shortly after the 40th anniversary of the opening of the Lodge Mission in 1970. It is intended to give a general idea of the vast scope of activities that this small but dynamic mission engaged in during its first five years when I served there as Henry Cabot Lodge's only assistant. I especially wanted to give an impression of our reporting mission to the Department of State, although it must be born in mind that a good deal of the subject matter we dealt with was often highly classified. As Cabot Lodge made only 14 official visits to Rome during my five-year tour, one will realize that he spent only about five to six weeks in Rome each year. While not accredited diplomatically to the Holy See, I in reality acted as a *chargé d'affaires* during the lengthy periods when Lodge was not there and it fell to me to carry on the heavy workload. My only assistance came from Kathy Astala, an amazingly qualified Foreign Service secretary who had previously worked for the Ambassador to Italy. In addition to her deep knowledge of Italy and its people, she also had an outstanding command of the language. We worked together cooperatively during my entire tour and to her goes much credit for the smooth and efficient running of the mission.

Given my conviction that the Lodge Mission was a small but important chapter in American foreign affairs, and in the case of the Vatican, was a major chapter indeed, I felt compelled to put some of its history into print. By now I am surely the only person living with an overall knowledge of the work we did. Knowing that there may be considerable interest in the broader public about the inside nature of the Vatican, I have aimed the book at a more general public, avoiding too heavy a dose of history and limiting the political side to issues in which our mission was directly involved or to which we contributed. To give proper focus, I have also included a brief history of our early relations with the Holy See and their many vicissitudes.

The success of the mission and its utility to the U.S. Government was demonstrated by the fact that after 14 years the White House decided to raise it to full diplomatic status. Notwithstanding this rise in official status, it would be hard to imagine that the current embassy is dealing with matters more significant than did our low-cost, miniscule operation hidden away in a discreet office in Rome. Of course, the reasons for raising our small mission to full embassy status were clearly as concerned with domestic American politics as with any question of diplomatic utility. The desire to satisfy the wishes of our large and influential Roman Catholic population were never far from the minds of those in Washington.

I

A Vaticanologist is Born

My assignment to the Vatican began as an office joke at the American Embassy in Belgrade where I was working as a second secretary in the political section. The White House announcement on June 5, 1970, that President Nixon would be sending Henry Cabot Lodge to the Vatican from time to time contained the ancillary comment that a Foreign Service Officer would be assigned to assist Ambassador Lodge. A distinguished public servant, Lodge had served as a Massachusetts Senator, Republican Vice-Presidential candidate, and Ambassador to the United Nations and the Republic of Vietnam. He was a man held in high regard.

The very idea of an American diplomat barrelling around the Vatican—a place whose name was as great as was our ignorance about it—unleashed days of amusing and flighty speculation in the political section of Embassy Belgrade about how this unique colleague might conduct himself, how he might be required to dress, act, speak, and in general, live. The thought of our man blithely discussing fine points of theology in his impeccable high-school Latin with a group of venerable cardinals was one of the main tableaux of our wild fancies.

I was just finishing three fascinating years in Yugoslavia and was expecting to be transferred to another overseas assignment in August. I would be leaving Yugoslavia during a moment of great optimism and hope for a more democratic and richer future. The normally impenetrable personnel office at the Department of State in Washington had informed me the previous November that they had tentatively slated me to be consul in Florence; this thought did not greatly pain me. Lulled by the idea of becoming at the minimum a modern-day renaissance man, living in a splendid Florentine palazzo, I was understandably shocked to learn in April that at the express request of Burke Elbrick, our previous ambassador to Yugoslavia who had been transferred to Brazil, I was to go to Rio de Janeiro. While I was perfectly pleased to go to Rio and work with Elbrick, I doubted this would happen as he had been the victim of a kidnap plot the previous fall, and I felt certain that he would, following normal practice in such cases, shortly be transferred out of Rio de Janeiro.

An exchange of letters confirmed that Elbrick had indeed requested my transfer to Rio. Then another bombshell hit: Elbrick was rushed to Washington for a series of delicate operations to correct some of the serious injuries he had suffered when he was dragged from his car and beaten during the kidnapping. From his hospital bed and between operations he most considerately cabled me to say that he doubted that he would be remaining much longer in Brazil and that I should be guided accordingly about my assignment.

On the basis of Elbrick's telegram, our new ambassador in Belgrade, Bill Leonhart, and his Deputy Chief of Mission, Tom Enders, interceded for me and got my Rio assignment broken.

At this point I was up for grabs at a moment when most good assignments had been given out—except for one as it turned out. A few days later Tom Enders called me into his office to ask if I had any objections to going on assignment to Rome. Being reasonably sound of mind, I said that I hadn't. He then told me that Washington had called to say that I was being considered for the position of assistant to Henry Cabot Lodge, and that if everything worked out all right I would be sent to Rome for one month's temporary duty "on approval." Should Lodge find me acceptable after this "honeymoon," I would have the job.

The news was so overwhelmingly joyful that I burst into peals of laughter. After giving my wife the news that evening, I went next-door to the ambassador's swimming pool for my daily swim.

On June 24, the feast of St. John and name day of Pope Paul VI, therefore a Vatican holiday, I arrived by plane in Rome and was met by Dick Christiansen, the embassy officer who had been keeping an unofficial eye on the Vatican, along with his heavier duties connected mainly with following the antics of the Italian Christian Democratic Party. Dick drove me to the Hotel delle Legazioni, where I stayed for about two weeks. As is so happily often the case in Italy, the food was good and I remember mealtime being enlivened by the manoeuvres of Mario, a tall, decorative waiter who mixed an unusually delicious salad.

Dick suggested that I get my feet wet immediately in the Vatican world. On the night of my arrival he took me to an animated cocktail party at the flat of Anthony Snellgrove, the First Secretary of the British Legation to the Holy See. It was so to speak, a baptism of champagne! The party turned out to be thoroughly enjoyable and also a useful introduction into the mysterious world of the Vatican. The atmosphere varied somewhat from the typical diplomatic affairs I had been used to: lots of clergy, many of the ladies were nuns dressed in conservative but not overly ecclesiastical suits, lots of Church talk. Quite a number of important officials of the Roman Curia, the central governing body of the entire Catholic Church who would shortly become important contacts for my work, were there that evening. I owe Tony, who was one of the best-informed diplomats at the Holy See, a big debt for smoothing my introduction to the many intricacies and complexities of the Vatican over the coming months.

My first days in Rome were given over to getting acquainted in the embassy, meeting a few key, working-level officials at the Vatican, and generally familiarizing myself with Rome, which I had previously only visited briefly. The Department of State's initial idea was that I would serve normally in the political section of the embassy, as did Dick Christiansen, and would shift over to be Lodge's assistant only when he was visiting Rome officially, presumably about three or four visits a year for stays of up to three weeks each. During Lodge's visits, we agreed with the Vatican that we would set up a small office in a suite at Rome's elegant and traditional Grand Hotel. In the discussions in Washington leading up to the agreement to have Lodge visit the Vatican, the Holy See had insisted that we respect its requirement that missions dealing with the Holy See be physically independent from embassies accredited to Italy. As we were to learn shortly, the Holy See takes great pains to demonstrate without the slightest doubt that they have nothing whatsoever to do with Italy. Totally distinct and independent!

Ambassador and Mrs. Lodge arrived at 1 a.m. on July 1, a strangely late hour for a singularly diurnal man. Despite having just completed a long and fatiguing journey, I found him and his lovely wife Emily extremely agreeable, an impression I was glad to find valid throughout the entire five years we worked together. On later visits, he wisely opted to break his trip with a Paris or London stopover.

After two agreeable weeks of living at the Hotel delle Legazioni, just off Piazza Barbarini, the embassy's Economic Minister offered me the use of his sumptuous apartment near the Villa Borghese while he went on home leave to the United States. All the top staff of the embassy, except the ambassador who resided in the Villa La Pariola, were housed in this splendid early 20th century villa. Lou and Virginia Boochever had one of the finest, higher-up apartments, which came equipped with Signor Yamani, an exceptionally distinguished looking Ethiopian butler. Yamani, who was the only servant in the house, had the distinct disadvantage that his culinary skills did not extend beyond preparing a simple breakfast. After a week of living at the Boochever's, I was walking down the via Veneto near the embassy with a colleague when Yamani, with an Ethiopian friend of his, passed nearby and greeted me. My friend asked if that distinguished, well-dressed gentleman were perhaps the Ethiopian ambassador. He was startled when I told him that, no, he was the Boochever's butler.

At the Grand Hotel, we took a two-room suite, one room for Lodge's office and the other for our Foreign Service secretary, Kathy Astala and myself.

Shortly after setting up our office for Lodge's first visit, President Tito of Yugoslavia arrived on a state visit to Italy and the Vatican. This pleasure- loving communist dictator stayed in the Grand Hotel. The morning of his departure for the Vatican, I just happened to take the back elevator to the ground floor, and when the door opened, whom did I see but Tito and his much younger wife Jovanka getting ready to enter their motorcade. They were dressed like resplendent Catholic sovereigns: Tito in white tie and decorations with a silk top hat and Jovanka in long black dress and mantilla. Since I had recently been assigned in Belgrade and knew the Titos slightly, I went up to them and started a conversation in Serbo-Croatian, commenting on how splendid they looked. Tito responded with a somewhat sheepish smile, probably feeling that dressed like a lord he was seriously betraying his avowed communist principles.

A few days after the Tito visit, an official of the pope's household told me that Tito had seemed awed with the splendour of the Vatican Palace and gave the impression of being a little schoolboy. This was seemingly not a strange reaction as the Vatican is indeed heavy with physical beauty as well as powerful historic associations. It is an overwhelmingly awesome place indeed. The word in the Vatican was that Winston Churchill was one of the few great men who were not visibly awed during his visit to see the Pope.

Ambassador Lodge remained in Rome for the whole month of July and we fulfilled a very heavy schedule of calling on a vast array of top Vatican officials. Our first audience with Pope Paul VI was on July 4, both to meet him and to discuss a wide range of issues of concern to the U.S. Government. High on our list were the questions of improving contact with American prisoners of war being held in North Vietnam and curtailing the flow of heroin through France and Italy, which were at that time the major points of entry of drugs into Europe and in many cases onward to the United States.

Although the Pope spoke serviceable English, Lodge decided to conduct this and all subsequent discussions in French, a language that he had learned to perfection during his boyhood school days in Paris before World War I. Lodge's mother had been widowed at an early age and she moved to Paris where for several years she raised her three children. Astonishingly, many of Lodge's prominent European contacts dated from those early days before World War I when he had studied at an avant-garde, elite school.

After the third week of working together, I hazarded to ask Lodge how he felt about my being formally assigned as his assistant. Much to my relief, he assured me that he would be pleased to have me stay on for a normal assignment as his assistant, and he agreed to take steps to make that a reality. As a result I was assigned initially for three years to the Lodge mission, a tour that was eventually extended for an additional two years at Lodge's request. The White House and the Vatican had agreed that Lodge could use his courtesy title of ambassador and that he would be called the president's special envoy to the Vatican. Although the Italians gave me courtesy diplomatic status, I operated officially only under the somewhat ambiguous, non-diplomatic title of "assistant to the special envoy." And with these two titles we both remained.

Quite obviously our mission had no professional interest in the religious activities of the Holy See or in the Church per se. What we wished to take fullest advantage of was the Holy See's genuinely impressive storehouse of information on political and social events worldwide. During Lodge's first visit and my initial contacts, it quickly became clear that the Vatican officials were prepared to share this information. In return, we were to respect the Vatican's desire for discretion. Any violation of trust from our side could result in the Vatican slamming shut the door that we had just begun to pry open. Over the five years that I served in Rome we made every effort, and in general succeeded, in demonstrating unequivocally to our hosts that we could be relied upon to keep our mouths firmly shut.

During the first crucial month, we concentrated on calling on the top Vatican cardinals, the heads of the Sacred Congregations or ministries dealing with such matters as the appointment of bishops, Catholic education, and the clergy. Cardinal John Wright, a jolly Irish-American from Boston, and the first American cardinal to serve in the Roman Curia, headed the Sacred Congregation for the Clergy. I had met the cardinal a few days after my arrival at a birthday party given for him in a historic villa outside Rome by Mickey Wilson, a well-informed and very useful British Catholic journalist. I first encountered Cardinal Wright sitting by the swimming pool in a white silk sport short with large red blotches on it. This brilliant, rotund man told me that he had bought the shirt, which he considered properly "cardinalizio", at a stall in a public market near his house.

The villa had been built by Julius II, the last Pope to personally command his armies. When he moved among his frequently cursing soldiers his typical comment was, "I absolve you my sons; you're fighting for the Lord." Incidentally, Julius used this house for a rest stop on his way back to Rome from his visits to the North. Being much more discrete than his predecessor Alexander VI (Borgia), he met his many mistresses at the villa rather than at the Vatican. Following a night in good female company Julius would make his way triumphantly back to the Vatican in the morning.

We were particularly interested in establishing contact with the many new departments that had been set up in the Vatican to deal with a wide range of modern issues, including relations with non-Catholics, with other religions, with non-believers, etc. The Commission for Justice and Peace was high on our list, and we came to relay heavily on its dynamic American secretary, Monsignor Joe Gremillion from Louisiana. The Archbishop of Vienna, Cardinal Koenig, a man of impressive intellect, dedication, and political savvy, dealt with the world of official atheism. Cardinal Willibrands toiled tirelessly in the vineyard of ecumenism, as did his inspiring boss Pope Paul.

After Lodge's first departure our secretary and I moved back to our discreet office on the fourth floor of Palazzo Margherita, the American Embassy in Rome. This imposing palazzo was the former home of Queen Margherita of Italy, who lived there following the assassination of her husband King Umberto I. From the time of the Renaissance, the palace been part of the Villa Ludovisi, one of central Rome's greatest princely estates. In the late 19th century Prince Ludovisi decided to subdivide his vast gardens and develop what became the area around via Veneto. This destructive act earned Ludovisi the opprobrium of Gregorovius, the great German historian of Rome. Once when the two met, Prince Ludovisi invited Gregorovius to lunch with him, to which the German replied that he would never sit down with a man who had destroyed his family's patrimony.

Following the second Lodge visit later in 1970, the Vatican noted that they would be most pleased if we could maintain our offices permanently outside the embassy. After discussions with the powers-that-be in Washington, we agreed to keep our suite on a full-time basis at the Grand Hotel. Needless to say, this was an expensive expedient, which the normally parsimonious U.S. Government managed to swallow in the case of Cabot Lodge.

After another year of looking at the bills in the guise of a taxpayer, I asked Lodge if it wouldn't be more practical to find office spaces in a normal office building. After more time than should have been necessary, I was authorized to find suitable accommodations and managed to locate a glorious suite of offices for only a fraction of what we were paying at the Grand Hotel. Our monthly rent dropped from $2,400 a month to $700, and for a much superior and more functional office. The offices were on the fourth floor of a 1900 vintage building just behind Villa Medici, the French Academy's headquarters in Rome. The view was breathtaking, somewhat better than the famous view from the roof of the Hotel Hassler that was just below us. One could see the entire sweep of Rome spread out at our feet, from Monte Mario on the right to Trastevere on the left, with St. Peter's smack in the middle. For the first few weeks it sometimes seemed tempting to stop working and just look out the window to enjoy such a captivating view spread out before us.

Ironically, we formally opened the new offices on May 20, 1974, very close to President Nixon's resignation date. This gesture was warmly welcomed in the Vatican, where it was seen as evidence of the United States' intention to continue its new permanent relationship with the Holy See. Our address at via di Porta Pinciana 4 was a new mini-star in the constellation of missions dealing with the Vatican and soon became an accepted meeting place for our many visitors and contacts. Embassy Rome was authorized to purchase us all the necessary furnishings in tasteful modern designs. I worked with the State Department's Historian and several archives in Rome, including the Vatican Secret Archives, to find suitable old photographs of former U.S. diplomats to the Papal States, views of buildings where our earlier missions had been housed, and photographs of significant documents in the history of our relations with the Vatican. For example, I found the copy of a letter of accreditation from President Abraham Lincoln in the Vatican Archives. When I visited our new American Embassy to the Holy See on the Aventine I was pleased to see that the historic items I had located were still decorating the walls of that mission.

During my entire five year stay in Rome our mission also kept its office spaces at the embassy. This was essential for storing our soon-to-become voluminous classified files. Since our operation was as much an appendage of the White House as it was of the State Department, we also generated and received a considerable amount of limited distribution communications. In fact, some of our more sensitive telegrams, especially concerning the Vietnam War, went only to the White House. Our routine communications went from Embassy Rome to the State Department or vice-versa, but I had authorization to approve all communications without reference to the embassy. Notwithstanding, I did from time to time avail myself of the vast experience of men at the embassy like Ambassador Graham Martin, Minister Wells Stabler, and Minister Bob Beaudry. From time to time we sent and received sensitive messages through CIA back channels.

Our normal working day usually began with a visit to our small offices on the top of the American Embassy to Italy, where we went through the vast daily take of telegrams, dispatches, and other correspondence. Since the bulk of this was classified either Confidential or Secret we were obliged to store it in our files at the embassy. After this effort was finished we took the short walk to our new offices about five blocks away. There were received frequent visitors and drafted up the day's outgoing correspondence. In general I went to the Vatican about three times a week for conversations or lunches with my contacts in a variety of local restaurants. Since we only had a car and driver available when Cabot Lodge was in town, I generally took a taxi or even walked to the Vatican.

Henry Kissinger, as a close friend of Ambassador Lodge and as an intellectual, seemed to find the workings of the Vatican very fascinating and therefore took a special interest in the Lodge Mission. In general, however, our contact in the National Security Council was Alexander Haig. During two of my official visits to Washington, I was allowed the most enjoyable privilege of using Al Haig's office for the several hours that I worked in the White House. Our back up at State was normally the Bureau of European Affairs, more generally the Italian Desk therein.

One of the great pleasures of my assignment to the Vatican was the warm personal relationship that developed between Ambassador and Mrs. Lodge and me and my family. I was most fortunate to come into Lodge's orbit at a time when he was virtually retired from active public life and he had ample free time just to talk with me and discuss a wide variety of fascinating topics. Lodge was something of a walking history book for just about everything of importance that had happened in the 20th century. His early memories of contacts with his famous grandfather, Senator Henry Cabot Lodge of Massachusetts, and even ex-President Teddy Roosevelt, gave him access to important events that took place even before his birth in 1902. In addition, with a godfather like Teddy Roosevelt, he had extremely impressive and enviable contacts from his earliest days. Lodge was a public-spirited and dedicated member of the traditional Eastern Establishment with a broad exposure to the wider world and an excellent grounding in foreign languages. His French was flawless and his German and Spanish quite serviceable.

One of Lodge's earliest foreign tasks had been to interview the new Italian dictator Benito Mussolini in Rome for the *Boston Transcript*, where he had his first serious job as a reporter. When the door to the Duce's office in the Palazzo Venezia was opened, Lodge was obliged to approach the august presence by crossing the enormous room on a diagonal path toward the desk where Mussolini sat awaiting him with a scowl on his pugnacious face. Not intimidated as was expected, Lodge advanced to undertake his interview. During this visit Lodge met one of the Duce's young secretaries, Leonardo Vittetti, who with his American wife remained friends with the Lodges until his return as special envoy.

While on their periodic visits to Rome, the Lodges took full advantage of the rich cultural opportunities of the city and the surrounding countryside. The ambassador kept himself in good physical condition and occasionally enjoyed a relaxing swim at the pool of Villa Taverna, the embassy residence in Rome. He also took frequent culturally oriented walks in the Roman Campagna with a circle of interesting friends, most of whom he had known for many years. We all made good use of our relations with the Vatican to arrange to see many monuments and private art collections not open to the general public.

The Lodges always arrived in Rome with a large suitcase crammed full of books that they read voraciously during their visits, usually propped up in bed at their suite in the Grand Hotel. History and biography were Lodge's great loves, and he had an impressive knowledge of European and American history. His contacts were vast almost beyond belief, especially from his days as American Ambassador to the United Nations under President Eisenhower. It was also surprising how well the Italians knew him. Wherever he went he usually received a friendly greeting by large numbers of people. It was clear that his personal dignity, impressive good looks, and decency made a lasting impression on people in many countries.

After five years in Rome I departed as the U.S. Government's only Vaticanologist, an *avis raris* if there ever was one in the American Foreign Service. In the 35 years that have elapsed since I left, no doubt a large new crop of Vatican experts has been trained. Given the likelihood of the Vatican's continuing to exist for many more years, becoming a Vaticanologist by a strange quirk of history now seems like a more solid career choice than the once very popular specialty of Sovietologist.

I saw the Lodges several times after leaving the Vatican job in 1975. Once just as the Republicans were gearing up to choose their candidate for the 1980 presidential elections, Lodge came in and said to us, "Guess who they're talking about as a possible Republican candidate?" "Who?" asked Mrs. Lodge. "George Bush" replied Lodge. "You've got to be joking, said Mrs. Lodge. "Why there's nothing to him. You see him from the front, then from the side, and there's just nothing there." And this was the comment from a long-time friend of the Bush family. God only knows what Mrs. Lodge would have thought of George W.

NOTE 1: It is useful to note that there are currently two categories of episcopal rank in the Catholic Church: residential (arch)bishops and titular (arch)bishops. As the name implies, the former are in charge of actual physical dioceses such as San Francisco, Paris, or the many others. Clergy of episcopal rank who do not head residential dioceses can be found among the auxilliaries to the residential bishops, the heads of the Holy See's diplomatic missions, and the many higher-ranking officials of the Roman Curia. All titular bishops are assigned a city name that formerly was a residential diocese but ceased to be one, usually many centuries ago. Most of this diocese, like the see of Carthage, is in lands now generally ruled by Muslims. These have been designated titular sees since 1882, before that time they were called *in partibus infidelium* or in the land of the infidels, which explains it all.

NOTE 2: Throughout this book you will frequently find the title monsignor; therefore, a proper definition is in order. There are currently two uses of the honorific title of monsignor: one is as a normal priest in any place who has been designated by the Holy Father as an honorary participant in the Pontifical Household. This gives the holder a rank just above a normal priest. The other is the use as a title of honor for persons of Episcopal or Archepiscopal rank. When a priest with the title of monsignor comes to Rome he is normally allowed to participate in ceremonies at St. Peter's Basilica.

II

A Relationship Grows—Slowly

The adjective that best describes the 213-year relationship between the United States and the Papacy is erratic. Starting with consular relations in 1797, the ties only rose to diplomatic status in 1848. To complicate matters further, diplomatic relations were suspended but not broken in 1868, and they were not resumed until 1984, when President Reagan sent his friend and financial advisor, William Wilson, as his fully accredited Ambassador to the Holy See. A few non-diplomatic special envoys and an informal following of what were called Vatican affairs by an officer in the political section of the American Embassy to Italy perforated this 116-year hiatus.

In reality, our relationship with the Holy See began in Paris in 1782, when our first diplomat, Benjamin Franklin, engaged in a series of conversations and contacts with Archbishop Doria Pamphili, the Papal Nuncio, mainly on matters concerning the future status of the Catholic Church in our new republic. For a people firmly convinced of the reality of the separation of state and church it may seem surprising that Benjamin Franklin had taken such an interest in the future of the Catholic Church in our infant country. But, he did as it developed.

Our formalized ties with the Papal States began in 1797 with the establishment of consular relations. The initiative for this step was not taken by the U.S. Government but by Giovanni

Battista Sartori, a Roman citizen, who wrote to Robert Morris, the Superintendent of Finances in the American Revolution, offering his services as consul in Rome. One cannot know for certain what prompted Sartori to make his offer, but one can speculate that it may have had something to do with his personal politics as well as self-interest. In any case, his offer was accepted and President John Adams named him as America's first consul in Rome. When the Roman Republic was established in 1798 under revolutionary French auspices, Sartori pressed the United States to recognize the new radical government. This would seem a clear demonstration that his ideological sympathies lay with the Enlightenment and republicanism. During the brief lifespan of the Roman Republic, Sartori acquired some confiscated papal lands, lands that he subsequently lost. In 1800 Sartori moved to the United States, leaving his brother Vicenzo in charge of the consulate in Rome, and he never returned to his native country. In spite of his seemingly strong republican views, Sartori was obviously not *persona non grata* with the Papal authorities, as he was named Consul General of the States of the Church in the United States in 1829, a position he exercised from his residence in Trenton, New Jersey.

Nothing is know of Sartori's early life but it is possible that he belonged to that Sartori family which formed part of the minor Roman nobility. These families frequently furnished lay functionaries for the Papal bureaucracy. Sartori may have been a reform-minded younger member of the family, the remainder of which continued on good relations with the authorities. It must be remembered that during the period we are considering it was quite fashionable to be interested in the new country across the oceans, and to be informed about its system and recent history. This could explain Sartori's personal history in the United States..

The second consul, named in 1823, was also a Roman, Felice Cicognani, a young lawyer serving the Papal Government. During this period, the work of the consulate consisted mainly of shipping matters and the care of the small but growing number of Americans visiting Rome. Cicognani managed to arrange very favorable conditions for American shipping in the Papal ports of Civitavecchia and Ancona, and the American Government reciprocated these terms for Papal vessels visiting American ports. Sadly, the volume of trade never reached very impressive levels. The growth in the number of Americans visiting and residing in Rome was substantial, however, and pressure grew among Americans to have one of their own citizens serve as consul in Rome. This pressure resulted in the naming in 1837 of George Washington Greene as the first American citizen consul, and in relieving Cicognani. Secretary of State John Forsyth made clear, however, that there was no dissatisfaction whatsoever with Cigognani's services, merely an understandable desire to have an American citizen in Rome.

The enthusiasm of Americans in Rome for having an American consul was short-lived, as they soon began to complain of Greene's practice of charging exorbitant fees for his consular services. This unleashed a row between the consul and his supporters in the United States and his detractors in Rome and elsewhere. The nub of the problem seemed to be the fact that at that time American consuls received no salary; their only income came from the somewhat arbitrarily set fees they collected for their services.

Greene protested to Washington that as a grandson of General Nathaniel Greene, to whom the republic owed so much, it would be only correct to grant him an established salary. Despite a large number of supporters both in the U.S. and Rome, nothing came of Greene's approach to Washington for a regular salary. It would be only toward the end of the 19th century that official salaries were established for American consular officers. The last straw in the battle against Greene was a complaint signed by seven Americans in Rome, alleging that American artists had to seek help from the British Consul in Rome to obtain studios and that Greene was demanding unjustifiable fees for shipping their art works back to the United States from Rome. Secretary of State Daniel Webster reacted to these rapidly accumulating complaints by removing Greene from his consulship.

The next consul was Nicholas Brown, who served only four years, from mid-1849. Brown witnessed the installation of the short-lived Second Roman Republic, that flourished briefly under the leadership of the eminent literary figure Giuseppe Mazzini. The event of the republic put an end to Pope Pius IX's short flirtation with liberalism and he was forced to flee to the Kingdom of Naples in the bottom of the Spanish Ambassador's carriage. Brown sent a series of very descriptive dispatches covering the main events of the revolutionary process underway before his eyes. While he shied away from offering American recognition to the republic, he did offer his rather florid congratulations to the foreign minister and attended a thanksgiving service for the new government. When the republic fell following the intervention of French troops, Brown offered his resignation to President Zachary Taylor. Unbeknown to Brown, his resignation crossed with the Department of State's new appointment of William Carroll Sanders as his successor. Brown's last act for the fallen republic was to smuggle out of Rome an ex-minister of the defunct republic, Pietro Sterbini, disguised as his servant.

Pius IX had a number of characteristics that led his contemporaries to hope that he would bring a fresh breath of air to the stale papal world in the form of more liberal ideas. He was the first Pope to have travelled outside Europe, having visited Latin America while on a papal visitation to that distant continent. At 54, he was the youngest Pope in memory. He clearly had a soft spot in his heart for the United States, and was instrumental in setting up the North American College, the headquarters of American clergy in Rome. As its seat he offered a beautiful abandoned convent near the Fountain of Trevi to the college, which they still own. As a very special honor, one evening he attended a jolly dinner with the American religious colony.

An amusing historical incident occurred during the time when Pius IX was in exile at Naples. One day when the Pope was visiting the King and Queen of Naples at their royal palace near the port of Gaeta, the American *Chargé d'Affaires* at Naples, John Rowan, paid a call at the palace. At that time the U.S. warship, the *USS Constitution*, was visiting Gaeta. When King Ferdinando asked if he could visit the ship, Rowan readily agreed and he also felt obliged to ask the Pope to come along. Thus, in a sense a Pope visited U.S. territory for the first time. Captain John

Gwinn welcomed his regal guests aboard, although in reality this was against his standing instructions, which were for the U.S. to remain strictly neutral in the ongoing disputes between the revolutionaries and the two "crowned heads."

Another incident involving the U.S. Navy took place about ten years later when an American ship briefly joined other ships from European powers that were patrolling the Papal coastline near Rome to help protect the Papal States from the Italian insurgents. Following this short call a young American midshipman was left at Civitavecchia, the main papal port, for six months to study the workings of the papal navy, which for some reason seemed to have impressed the young man's naval superiors. As a result of the midshipman's report the U.S. Navy decided to adopt for their own use the gunnery manual of the Papal Navy!

The first fully accredited American diplomat to the Holy See was the hapless Jacob Martin of North Carolina, who arrived in Rome in August 1848 with letters of credence as *chargé d'affaires* from President James Polk. Polk had taken the decision to establish full diplomatic relations in opposition to public opinion and most of the Congress. In his opinion the election of a pope who promised to be a liberal and the growing importance of the Papal States to America justified such a move. Pope Pius IX, still in his modernizing phase, received Martin on August 19, and expressed his deep pleasure at the occasion. Martin was delighted with the honors he received during his presentation of credentials ceremony and with the favorable way his presence was discussed in the official papal gazette. Martin's glory was short-lived, however, for only three weeks after his arrival, he was dead on August 26 from a stroke, following a bout with one of Rome's ever-prevalent fevers. As an economy gesture, so typical and incumbent on American diplomats then as now, he had taken lodging in a ground floor, back room in the down-market Hotel Serny on the Piazza di Spagna. It was in this unpretentious and insalubrious room where he was found dead.

The story does not end there. Martin was buried in the Testaccio Cemetery along the Aurelian Wall, a burial ground reserved for non-Catholics. His funeral procession was enriched by a troop of Papal Dragoons. The cost of the headstone placed on his grave exceeded the State Department's maximum allowance of $100 by $10. Typical of the parsimonious State Department, a debate was carried on by diplomatic dispatch for over a year on how to recover the excess $10! While in Rome, I located Martin's grave, cleaned it up, and put flowers on it each August 26, a custom that I understand was continued for at least some years after my departure.

After an interval of eight months Lewis Cass, Jr. arrived to replace Martin as *Chargé d'Affaires*, a position that was raised to full Minister Resident in 1854. Cass was the son of a diplomat who later became Secretary of State, which created the unique circumstance of Lewis Cass, Jr. sending official correspondence to Lewis Cass, Sr. There was considerable friction between Cass and Consul Brown over the true nature of the republican government that had been set up in the Papal States, particularly over whether or not the U.S. should accord recognition. In the end, Brown left and Cass finally presented his credentials to the Pope, who had by that time returned from his exile in the Kingdom of Naples.

Three more consuls served under Cass; despite this there was a four-year period during which no consul was in place. An embarrassing bilateral event took place in 1853 when the Pope sent Archbishop Bedini to the U.S. to visit the American Catholic hierarchy. The president and other top officials warmly received Bedini. During these encounters Bedini sounded out the receptivity of the U.S. to receive a papal nuncio. The proposal did not receive a warm welcome, but Bedini did receive a rather hot welcome from anti-Catholic and pro-Italian unification demonstrators.

The first indications that Congress might be looking with disfavor at having a mission accredited to the Papal States arose during the tenure of John P. Stockton, Minister Resident from 1858 to 1861. Congress was keenly aware that the days of papal government were probably numbered as the forces of the united Italy moved inexorably toward their final goal of conquering Rome. A bill to cut off funding—the preferred method of closing the Rome mission—was narrowly defeated. At the same time Stockton appealed to the Department to raise the level of his mission one notch to a full rank of minister plenipotentiary; his argument was that the representatives of most small countries like Nicaragua and Guatemala outranked him, the representative of the clearly more powerful United States.

Toward the end of his term Stockton also played a crucial role in having the exiled King of Naples transported in an American warship to Messina where the king encouraged his remaining loyal garrison to capitulate, therefore saving many lives that might otherwise have been lost in continuing a losing fight against overwhelming Italian odds.

During the American Civil War, agents of the Confederate States visited Rome in an attempt to urge the Papal States to recognize their rebellious government, all to no avail due to the efforts of the United States diplomatic representative at Rome, who frequently had to exhort the Papal Government to refuse entry to Confederate agents travelling on false passports. At that time only American passports authenticated by the legation in Rome were valid for travel in the Papal States. During his brief 15 months in Rome Minister Resident Richard M. Blatchford was informed indirectly by the Pope that His Holiness would be prepared to mediate a peace to terminate the American Civil War. Top Vatican officials expressed to the Minister their regret at any circumstance that might lead to a division of the United States, noting the great importance they attached to our remaining a strong and undivided nation.

The last American Minister to the Papal States was Rufus King, who spent much of his time trying to keep track of Confederate agents. He also made known the American Government's dissatisfaction over the fact that Pius IX had replied to a letter from Jefferson Davis, using his title of President of the Confederate States of America. The Papal Government made abundantly clear that this was a mere courtesy and in no way implied recognition. Somewhat later Jefferson Davis named Bishop Patrick Lynch of Charleston, South Carolina as his Confederate Commissioner to the States of the Church. Lynch visited several European capitals and made calls at the Vatican, which was scrupulous in receiving him exclusively in his capacity as a Catholic bishop.

Rufus King kept careful tabs on Lynch and was pleased to see that no Vatican official was giving anything approaching recognition to Lynch in his role as a representative of the Confederate States of America; they received him merely as a bishop at every instance. Cardinal Antonelli, the Secretary of State, assured King that the Holy See considered the Confederacy as a revolutionary state and that the Church only recognized border changes and new regimes after their existence had been solemnized in a formal treaty of peace with standing in international law. It's worth noting that the Vatican still scrupulously follows this policy in all instances. In the 1860s, the Vatican was staunchly opposed to the existence of slavery and the slave trade, which obviously did not put the Confederacy in a good light at Rome. In all King's discussions at the Vatican with the Pope and the descending hierarchy, it was amply clear that the Holy See was firmly on the side of the United States during the Civil War.

Even Robert E. Lee took part in the efforts to elicit papal support for the Confederate cause and for recognition of the Confederacy. After the Battle of Richmond, Lee wrote a personal letter to Pope Pius IX seeking his understanding. The Pope answered with a polite but totally noncommittal letter, which can still be found in the Vatican Archives.

King did, however, manage to earn a rebuke from the State Department for attending a reception given in Rome for the Archduke Maximilian and his wife Carlota, the new French-backed rulers of Mexico. King managed to turn his misfortune around shortly after when it became known that John Suratt, a suspect in the murder of President Lincoln, had been enrolled as a private in the Papal Zouaves. Despite the absence of an extradition treaty with the United States, the Papal Government agreed with King's request to have Suratt apprehended. This was agreed, but Suratt managed to escape his captors and flee into Tuscan territory, then to Naples, and finally to Alexandria, Egypt where he was captured by the good offices of the American Consul there and shipped back to the United States in an American Navy ship.

With the Papal States collapsing around his shoulders, the Pope gave some serious thought to the possibility of escape to a foreign refuge. The possibility of fleeing to the British colony of Malta was discussed discretely with the British Government. The Pope's minister of war, General Kanzler, and the Pope's private chaplain had several discussions with Rufus King on the possibility of the Pope even seeking haven in America. Kanzler asked that an American warship be added among those vessels of friendly powers that were waiting in the papal port of Civitavecchia, north of Rome. An American warship, the *USS Swatara*, was as a result dispatched to Civitavecchia, but Secretary of State Seward chided King for believing, merely on the basis of conversations with subordinates, that the Pope might actually be entertaining the idea of going to America. This was probably an unfair accusation on Seward's part as General Kanzler could not have been considered a "subordinate" official.

Shortly after, King learned from the American press that an effort was underway in the Congress to cut off funding for the legation in Rome. This threat turned out to be true, and shortly after, King was obliged to depart Rome without the customary letters of recall announcing his departure. No longer on salary, the humiliated King departed Rome unannounced, as the Papal States were entering their final stages of collapse. This, with the added pressure to the movement to cut off all funds for the legation at Rome, and the unfounded rumor that the Papal Government had ordered the American Protestant Church to be moved outside the walls of Rome, hastened his departure.

For the last year of papal rule only American Consul David Armstrong was assigned, and he managed to witness the conquest of Rome by the forces of the Kingdom of Italy. Armstrong remained in his post to serve under the first American Minister to the united Italy, George P. March.

One of the principal objectives of the *Risorgimento* was to establish the capital of Italy in Rome, historically the country's most important city even though it was smaller that Naples, at that time the largest city on the Italian peninsula and the third largest city in Europe. During the struggle to unite Italy the capital had first been moved from Turin to Florence, and then, when in 1870 the Pope's temporal power was terminated, the door was finally opened to move the government definitively to Rome. This was achieved only in 1874. Despite the fact that the pope lost all his political and temporal powers, Rome remained unquestionably the pope's city. All the great buildings and churches reminded one clearly of the previous millennium of papal rule and glory. Papal coats-of-arms and other symbols were everywhere. How could the new monarchy compete successfully in creating a new image of centrality in the city? In short, it didn't—very successfully.

In comparison to the King of Italy, the Pope continued to be the dominant personality of Rome; visitors came mainly to visit the center of Roman Catholicism and to see the Pope, rather than to admire the glories of the Italian Monarchy. To add to the irony, the king lived in the pope's former palace. To this day the pope continues to play the dominant role in the life of Rome. The situation is further aggravated by the fact that neither the monarchy nor the present republic have managed to create a physical presence in the city that begins to balance the monumental presence of the Church and its 1,900-year-long string of rulers. My view has long been that to put the capital of Italy in Rome was a great historical error and managed only to guarantee putting the secular rulers of Italy under the long shadow of the Church. Although the ties have weakened a good bit under the reigns of two non-Italian popes, and also due to the general movement of secularization, the burden of Papal Rome still hangs heavily over Italy.

The combined 70 years, first of consular and then diplomatic relations with the Papal States, had been highly useful in the protection of the interests of American citizens in the territory, covering the fast-moving political situation in Italy and fomenting trade. None of these considerations made an impact after 1868. In reality, the importance of the Pope beyond his role as the ruler of the Papal States—which obviously had ceased to exist—was completely lost on the American leadership at the time.

During the sixty years during which the United States maintained either a consulate or a legation or both in Rome, they were housed in a wide variety of buildings in the center of the city. For some years the consulate was in a back room of a British bank at the bottom of the Spanish Steps, where can now be found Babington's Tea-room.

From 1868 until the eve of World War II there were no formal relations between the United States and the Holy See. With the outbreak of hostilities in Europe in 1939, by mutual consent, it was decided that Myron Taylor would periodically visit the Vatican as Personal Representative of President Franklin D. Roosevelt. Mr. Taylor, who had the personal rank of ambassador, continued in this capacity until 1950. During this ten-year period he made eight visits to Rome, several during the time of actual hostilities. Mr. Taylor's deputy, Foreign Service Officer Harold Tittmann, was forced to move physically into the Vatican City when the United States formally entered the war against Italy; he remained there continuously until the Allied liberation of the city in 1944. Since the Italian Government strenuously objected to Tittmann living in the Vatican as a non-accredited diplomat, the State Department broke down and appointed him formally as *chargé d'affaires* to the Holy See. When Tittmann left the Vatican assignment in 1944 Franklin C. Gowen, another Foreign Service Officer who held the title of aide to Ambassador Myron C. Taylor, replaced him briefly.

Prior to sending Taylor to Rome there was some discussion in American political circles about the advantages of having an embassy to the Holy See. The fight against Godless communism, the crusade against the forces of Nazism and Fascism, and the ability to obtain valuable intelligence, were among them.

In 1950 President Harry Truman sent the name of General Mark Clark, hero of the liberation of Italy and Rome, to the Senate for confirmation as the first United States Ambassador to the Holy See. General Clark's nomination was unacceptable to the Senate, after several months of Senate inaction the White House felt forced to withdraw the nomination. An increase in the belief that a relationship with the Holy See violated traditional American principles of the separation of church and state and renewed fears that such ties could facilitate Catholic meddling in

American affairs acted against opening an embassy at that time. It was rumoured that Truman wanted and expected the Clark nomination to fail; he simply wanted to hold true to a promise made to Pius XII that after the war the U.S. Government would establish full diplomatic relations. The answer to this is moot.

The Taylor mission was then hastily closed in a manner that irritated the Vatican and for many years thereafter relations with the United States Embassy to Italy, which continued to follow Vatican affairs in a desultory manner, were quite cool. Things gradually improved somewhat up until 1970, when President Richard Nixon made the ground-breaking announcement that he planned to send Henry Cabot Lodge as his special envoy to the Vatican.

III

Ben Gives an Assist to the Church in America

What did Benjamin Franklin and Archbishop Doria Pamphili, the Papal Nuncio in France, have in common? Certainly it wasn't that one was a self-made man and a Dissenter from a modest background in faraway America and the other the scion of a Genoese-Roman princely family and soon to be a cardinal. No, it was to engage in a series of conversations over an extended period about the future of the American Catholic Church. Franklin mentions these contacts in his journals and in his autobiography but gives no specifics. A fuller record is available in the Secret Vatican Archives and in the archives of the Sacred Congregation for the Propagation of the Faith (Propaganda Fidei), the Vatican office that deals with missionary churches, which the American Church initially was.

Top posting in Paris attests to Nuncio Doria Pamphili's great experience and high ranking in the papal diplomatic service. His frequent dispatches, all in Italian, are terse, informative, and dry. Only his outing to witness the launch of the first Montgolfier balloon from the Champs de Mars released a spate of boyish enthusiasm in his dispatch detailing the social, technical, and colorful aspects of the event. Unlike today, Vatican diplomats before 1870 were representing a normal European power and they reported a wide range of information, from military matters to trade promotion.

Benjamin Franklin's crucial role in the attainment of American independence, in securing indispensable material aid from France, and in negotiating peace with Great Britain are all well known; his part in helping the Holy See set up an independent structure for the American Church has received little attention. Yet, this was probably the third most important item to occupy him from mid-1783 to late 1784.

When the Revolutionary War began only about 25,000 Roman Catholics lived in the Thirteen Colonies, mostly in Maryland and Pennsylvania, with a few in New York. There were no local bishops; control was under Bishop Richard Challoner in London, who carried the title of vicar apostolic. Then as now it was standard Vatican practice not to alter Church boundaries or governance in the absence of a signed peace treaty. Only when the outcome of the American war was obvious and the process of negotiating a peace treaty had gotten under way did the Holy See begin to consider ways to reorganize the Church in America and to discuss the matter with U.S. diplomats in Paris.

The Nuncio first mentions Franklin in a dispatch of December 16, 1776, when he reports "Dr. Franklin, the long-time agent of the Americans in London has arrived at Nantes and is expected shortly in Paris." Actually Franklin had arrived aboard the *Reprisal* on December 3 at Auray, a distance up the Breton Coast from Nantes. He reached Paris on December 21.

Doria Pamphili does not mention when he first met Dr. Franklin, but it is clear from his reporting that he saw his American colleague from time to time at court in Versailles and at other diplomatic functions. The first report of an actual meeting is in 1777 when the Nuncio had received a request from Cardinal Pallavicini, the Papal Secretary of State, saying that Pope Pius VI would like to have a copy of the Declaration of Independence and would the Nuncio please ask Dr. Franklin to provide one. This the Nuncio dutifully did. The series of meetings to discuss the Church in America, however, only began in 1783, after the Treaty of Paris of September 3, 1782, gave the Vatican a green light to move forward.

The Nuncio's reporting throughout the Revolutionary War gave detailed coverage to British naval and troop movements, and it is evident that he was privy to French intelligence in these areas. As an example, on October 4, 1779, he lists all the British ships in the harbor of Portsmouth, including names of their commanding officers and the number of cannons. His reporting of actual military engagements concentrates on French actions, particularly in the Caribbean theater, where names like de Grasse, d'Estaing, and Rochambeau are frequently mentioned. He also describes the activities of John Paul Jones, notably around Ireland, and the danger that this posed to Britain's hold over the Catholic Irish. Clearly our princely archbishop was very much at home with military matters.

On January 23, 1781, Franklin writes in his journal that he "had some conference with the Nuncio who seemed inclined to encourage American vessels to come to the ecclesiastical states, acquainting me they had two good ports to receive us, Città Vecchia and Ancona." He further noted that good business could be done at these ports, especially for American fish. The two aforementioned ports were in fact only opened to American shipping in 1784 when friendly relations officially began.

In a letter to his friend David Hartley, Franklin noted that he had heard that when he first presented his credentials as a minister plenipotentiary in 1779 the diplomats in Paris had decided not to return his calls. He disappointed their project, he writes, by visiting none of them. The Minister then observes that the "first civility is due from the old resident to the stranger and new-comer. My opinion, indeed, is good for nothing against custom, which I should have obeyed but for the circumstances that rendered it more prudent to avoid disputes and affronts, though at the hazard of being thought rude or singular." As the Nuncio reports, Franklin's understanding of what motivated the other diplomats in Paris was completely erroneous.

When word reached Paris that Franklin was to be given diplomatic status as a minister plenipotentiary, the diplomats at Paris did in fact meet to discuss how he should be received. The normal procedure at the French Court for receiving a new diplomat was extremely formal and costly. Contrary to what Franklin seemed to understand, and obviously no one ever properly informed him, his soon-to-be colleagues were keenly aware that he was operating on a seriously limited budget. They also appreciated that the new republic had neither the desire nor intention to fulfill many old world formalities; therefore, they were prepared to ease Franklin's situation and spare him any unnecessary embarrassment.

According to the Nuncio's report, the diplomatic corps realized that the American would be hard-pressed to fulfill the expected protocol for presenting credentials as a minister, hence they decided after considerable deliberation that Franklin's case should be governed by the more relaxed rules for a "visiting noblemen at court." This required only one carriage drawn by two horses rather than four. It also required our "minister/visiting nobleman" only to leave his card with the other chiefs-of-mission, a practice which did not oblige the others to reciprocate calls. Needless to say, other requirements involving domestic staff, footmen, grooms, etc. were ignored to accommodate Benjamin Franklin. He simply did not understand what had been done for him; one of the few times perhaps that he missed the point. Cardinal Pallavicini in Rome complimented the Nuncio for his role in helping to solve this heretofore unheard of diplomatic dilemma.

Franklin may have poked fun at European etiquette, but in one area he found European practice estimable. In his "Sketch of My Service to the United States" dated November 29, 1788, he wrote, "I must own, I did hope that, as it is customary in Europe to make some liberal provision for ministers when they return home from foreign service during which their absence is necessarily injurious to their private affairs, the Congress would at least have been kind enough to have shown their approbation of my conduct by a grant of some small tract of land in their western country, which might have been of use and some honor to my posterity." Sadly, modern Congresses still reflect a similar indifference and lack of gratitude toward former diplomats. As Franklin would have said, "*Le plus ça change.*"

Following the Peace of Paris the Nuncio engaged Franklin in earnest to explore ways to break the governance of the American Catholic Church out from under British control. The Vatican realized that the French were ideally placed to help in the matter and that the French Minister to the United States, the Chevalier de la Luzerne, was able to provide authentic information and guidance on circumstances in the new republic. What took place thereafter was a three-way discussion, involving Franklin and occasionally Adams on the American side, the Nuncio for the Vatican, and the Foreign Minister, the Comte de Vergennes, and the Bishop of Autun for the French._

From the Vatican's perspective the task ahead consisted of forming a legal groundwork for dealing with the United States on ecclesiastical matters, the naming of a leader for the American Catholic community, and the training of future American clergy. At this point the Sacred Congregation for the Propagation of the Faith comes into the picture, and Doria Pamphili's dispatches go to its head, Cardinal Antonelli.

Heretofore, the Church had been used to dealing with two distinct situations: either reasonably friendly Catholic powers like France, or rather hostile non-Catholic states ranging from Protestants to non-Christians. Naturally, the experience varied greatly from time and place. At the outset, the Vatican assumed the Americans would like to take a strong role in forging a more formal relationship. This might even result in a written agreement, although probably less formal than the concordats the Vatican was used to signing with traditional Catholic states.

The essential first step for Rome was to designate a cleric to reside in America with some episcopal powers, an indispensable factor for ordaining clergy and confirming youth. Realizing that the Vatican would soon be obliged to remove control of the American Church from London, the American clergy in 1783 petitioned Rome to name Father John Lewis as their superior. This was not to be, however, for on June 9, 1784, the Pope named John Carroll to be prefect apostolic and head of the missions in the United States. Pope Pius VI only decided to create the first full diocese in the United States on September 17, 1789, when he named John Carroll as Bishop of Baltimore. What, if anything, was Benjamin Franklin's role in the choice of Carroll?

John Carroll was born in Upper Marlborough, Maryland in 1735, the son of a prominent Catholic family established in the colony since the 17th century. He studied for the priesthood in Flanders and was ordained in 1769. He subsequently joined the Jesuit Order in 1771, but when the Pope suppressed that order in 1773, he returned as a secular priest to the American colonies and worked in Rock Creek, Maryland as a missionary. He and Franklin met in 1776 when the Continental Congress sent them together with Charles Carroll and Samuel Chase to Canada in an attempt to negotiate the neutrality of French Canadians during the Revolutionary War. The mission failed, as the Canadian Catholics were unwilling to join an enterprise with Protestants. Yet, there was a lasting result of Carroll's trip to Canada: Franklin's respect and friendship.

On July 28, 1783, the Nuncio advised Franklin, "It is well known that this arrangement (having the American Church under some one in London) can no longer exist." He went on to observe that it was essential for the Catholics to have a cleric with episcopal powers, and asked that Franklin seek the approval of Congress for the Holy See to proceed with the designation of a suitable American priest and the choice of a city in North America as his see. The Nuncio opined that it was best not to name a full bishop at the outset, as this would probably require the naming of a foreigner. Naming an apostolic vicar or apostolic prefect, prelates with partial episcopal powers, would be the best way to start. If it turned out that no appropriate American were available, Congress should allow the candidate to be chosen from among the subjects of a foreign power most friendly to the United States. (Elsewhere the Nuncio had revealed his superiors' ignorance of the state of the Church in America and the belief that no suitable candidate for leadership could be found there.)

The desire of the Holy See to sound out Congress probably stemmed from their general experience and practice of leaving no major question unanswered by highest authority, "in writing." Moreover, Doria Pamphili, in his professional astuteness, seemed to perceive that the American representatives were operating on a somewhat uncharted sea. The way America might act on one given matter gave no clear indication how it might act on a subsequent matter, even if the latter were of a seemingly similar nature. In some cases we might take a traditional course, in others a radical one. The Nuncio realized that for America there was often a total absence of precedent. For some time Doria Pamphili continued to press Franklin for Congress's approval, obviously considering it normal that the U.S. Government, like most governments his Church had dealings with, would wish to take an active role in deciding the future status of America's Catholics.

August and September 1783 were months of frequent discussions between Franklin and the Nuncio. In mid-August the Nuncio expressed his pleasure to Cardinal Pallavicini that the Pope valued and approved of the manner in which he conducted his contacts with Messrs. Adams and Franklin, "qualified Ministers Plenipotentiary of the new republic of the United States of North-America for the peace." He further reports, "On a recent occasion presented to me to see and speak to Mr. Franklin, I took advantage to inspire and impress on him, as I previously had done, the favorable impression made on our court by their (U.S.) desire to cooperate in the propagation and free exercise of the Roman Catholic faith in the domains of his new republic."

The previous two months of conversations were tied up in a detailed dispatch that Doria Pamphili sent to Rome on September 1, 1783. Included were three important attachments labeled A, B, and C. "A" was a note that the Nuncio had sent to Franklin outlining the questions at hand, "B" was Franklin's brief acknowledgment on "A", and "C" was Franklin's observations on what should be done. In "C" Dr. Franklin states his conviction that the "Court of Rome on its own could take all those measures useful to the Catholics of America without offense to the Constitution, and that the Congress will not fail to approve tacitly any choice of a French ecclesiastic that Propaganda Fidei, in concert with the Minister Plenipotentiary of United States, will make." This French prelate will reside permanently in France and have a suffragan in America. Franklin also recommends the training of Americans for the priesthood in France but not at seminaries where Englishmen are currently studying, which would not be acceptable. Finally, Franklin informed the Nuncio "it was absolutely useless to submit anything to Congress because their rules and the Constitution do not permit any involvement in religious affairs, this being reserved to the various states." Each state constitution, moreover, said Franklin, "is obliged to guarantee religious tolerance and protect the members of all religions in the free exercise of their faith as long as they do not trouble the public order."

In his dispatch of May 27, 1784, Doria Pamphili informed Rome that Franklin was favorable to naming the ex-Jesuit Carroll as vicar apostolic in Maryland. Franklin had told him about his mission to Canada with Carroll in 1776 as Commissioners of the Congress. (He probably didn't tell the Nuncio why the mission failed.) Clearly citing Franklin, the Nuncio reports that "this choice (Carroll) would be very pleasing to many members of Congress and in particular to Benjamin Franklin, who has strongly recommended him." It is clear from the context Doria Pamphili had been discussing Carroll with Franklin for some time.

In the above dispatch the Nuncio mentions that an attack of the "stones" had kept Franklin from attending the levee at Versailles and that he sent his grandson (Templeton Franklin) in his place. Since Doria Pamphili missed the grandson, he took the opportunity the following day to call on Franklin at his house in Passy for a chat.

The Vatican wasted no time, for on July 1, 1784, the Nuncio called Franklin to say that on his recommendation the Pope had appointed John Carroll (on June 9 in fact) as "superior of the Catholic clergy in America" with many powers of a bishop; and that Carroll would probably be made a bishop *in partibus* (what is today a titular bishop) before the end of the year. The Nuncio then asked whether it would be more convenient for Carroll to go to Santo Domingo or France for ordination by another bishop. Franklin replied that Quebec would be more convenient than either. The Nuncio then delicately asked whether its being an English province might not be offensive to us. Franklin told him there would be no problem if ordination did not place Carroll under the authority of Quebec, which the Nuncio assured him, would not be the case.

The other weighty matter that occupied much of the Nuncio's attention during this period was the question of training American priests. The Comte de Vergennes, the Bishop of Autun, and the Chevalier de la Luzerne through his dispatches from America, took an active part in these discussions. Autun, the French bishop responsible for Church benefices, initially suggested seminaries at St. Malo, Nantes, L'Orient or any other city close to the sea where they could meet seafarers from home, as possible localities to train American seminarians. Vergennes and the Bishop of Autun assured the Nuncio that they would undertake to find the necessary funds for training the Americans. The Nuncio praises Vergennes' dedication to the Church in the highest terms. Eventually a seminary in Bordeaux was chosen as the site for the study of eight to ten Americans, all expenses to be covered by the King of France. The Nuncio observed, perhaps ingenuously, that the presence of other English-speaking seminarians from the British Isles would make the integration of the Americans easier.

While the above program was being finalized the Pope agreed to fund two scholarships for Americans at the Collegio di Propaganda Fidei in Rome. In this regard, the Nuncio had met an American convert to Catholicism from Boston, John Thayer, who wished to study for the priesthood, and if Dr. Franklin had no objections he would send him to Rome to take up one of the Pope's scholarships. According to Franklin's journal the Nuncio must have had a change of heart about Thayer, whom he advised to stay in France. The Nuncio seemed to feel that Thayer's desire to convert his countrymen was if anything meaningless, since he knew little of his new religious belief. The Nuncio reported Franklin's "overwhelming gratitude and happiness and assurances that his republic would be very pleased to have two or three of its citizens as students in Rome, having a high opinion of the studies there."

On May 11, 1784, Congress finally issued the long-sought instructions to Dr. Franklin, which read as follows: "Resolved, that Doctor Franklin be desired to notify to the apostolic Nuncio at Versailles, that Congress will always be pleased to testify their respect to his Sovereign and State; but that the subject of his application to Doctor Franklin being purely spiritual it is without the jurisdiction and powers of Congress who have no authority to permit or refuse it, these powers being reserved to the several states individually." Franklin sent a copy of these instructions to the Nuncio under cover of his diplomatic note of August 18. When the Nuncio forwarded this long-awaited reply from Congress to his superiors in Rome they expressed surprise and satisfaction. There is a palpable feeling in all the correspondence between Rome and Paris of astonishment that a government could exist that was interested neither in meddling in religious affairs nor in hindering them.

This is almost certainly the first time in its long history that the Catholic Church had met with genuine religious freedom. Likewise, it was also probably their first experience in dealing with the separation of church and state. Clearly Franklin appreciated the American position on religious freedom but he certainly did not practice the separation of church and state to its fullest, even though he did appreciate that the Congress would not wish to become involved. We must remember that this was still a formative period for American constitutional law, a few years before the First Amendment and the debates surrounding its approval more fully clarified the policy. For his part, Pope Pius VI, later to suffer so much pain over church-state matters with Napoleon, reacted with deep surprise but great pleasure. The Church had never before encountered a state that was well disposed toward religion but disinterested in regulating it.

It is natural to assume that a man like the Nuncio, from a conservative Catholic background and representing the most traditional power in Europe, could have been distressed over the reality of the United States, a country formed by a rebellion against its legitimate prince and whose proclaimed republican principles left no room for kings, nobles, or established churches. While recognizing the inherent threat in the existence of such a republic the Holy See no doubt saw, like France and Spain, some advantages in supporting the Americans. More than any particular interest in helping the American cause per se, was an overriding interest in weakening the power of that arch-heretical country, Great Britain. Another hope might have been to give a breathing space to the Catholic Spanish colonies in America. There was also the possibility of Catholicism flourishing better in the new country free of British domination. In any case the gamble was made.

The Nuncio's final report on his contacts with Franklin is dated August 23, 1784. In it he forwards the instructions from Congress cited above and comments that, "It is not sure that the American Republic will with time continue to be grateful for the singular services and favors given them by France and they might fall into a revolution similar to Canada. It would be convenient to be satisfied with what one can get and for the future submit to what God will be good enough to grant." A more pessimistic—and prophetic—sentiment was reported at the same time by the Spanish Ambassador to France to his Foreign Minister in Madrid. The Conde de Floridablanca foresaw that "'this tiny infant republic' which we now aid in its birth may some day grow to be a colossus and turn on those who are now its benefactors." How true with Spain in 1898!

How important was Franklin's recommendation of John Carroll to be the local head of the American Church? Given that the American clergy, with Carroll's participation, had forwarded to Rome their recommendation that Father John Lewis be chosen as their head, there are no grounds for suspecting that the Holy See's choice would have fallen on Carroll had Franklin not strongly supported him. As the Nuncio was willing to accord Franklin considerable influence in American Church affairs, Franklin could just as easily have blocked Carroll's candidacy or proposed some one else. It's entirely likely, however, that Franklin did not know any other American priests. Therefore, it would seem safe to conclude that Franklin was uniquely responsible for Carroll ending up as the first Catholic bishop in the United States.

Thus ended a virtually unknown but rather interesting episode from the infancy of American diplomacy. As a new republic we were feeling our way in a new situation and the other powers were similarly groping along about how to cope with a radically new type of state. That a free-thinking, former Grand Master of the Masonic Lodge of Pennsylvania and Venerable of the Lodge of the Nine Sisters in Paris should have played such a clearly sympathetic role in the establishment of an independent Catholic Church in America is surprising; that he worked so well with such an unlikely counterpart as Archbishop Doria Pamphili is, if anything, intriguing.

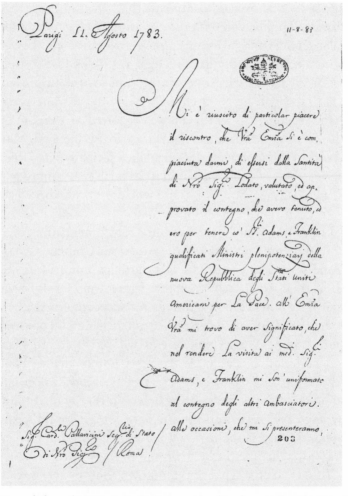

Dispatch from the Nuncio in Paris expressing his pleasure that the Pope is pleased with manner in which he is dealing with the American representatives

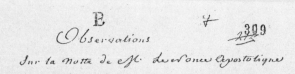

Benjamin Franklin's observations on the note from the Nuncio in Paris

Correspondence between Benjamin Franklin and the Nuncio advising that the Continental Congress could not become involved in regulating the Catholic Church in America.

IV

Historical Growth of Papal Power

Almost everyone is aware that the Pope is the head of the worldwide Roman Catholic Church. What is less generally known is that he is also the head of a sovereign entity called the Holy See, which is described later. This lesser known papal role developed over the centuries, stemming from the pope's former position as head of the Papal States, an independent state encompassing most of the central Italian peninsula. To better understand how this papal role developed, the following capsule history will prove helpful.

Beginning with St. Peter in the early 1st century, the popes were at first merely the bishops of Rome, the leaders of what was essentially a small but growing band of persecuted Christians. At best, these early Christians lived with the sufferance of the Roman authorities. Interestingly, the Romans did not persecute Christians due to their faith per se; as polytheists, the Romans were broad-minded about the religions of other peoples under their rule. Rather, the persecution of Christians arose from their refusal to take part in nominal sacrifices to the Roman emperors. In order to maintain their status, the Roman leaders felt they could not back down on this issue, and Christians were persecuted as a result. During the first 300 years of the Papacy, Christians in Rome lived a precarious existence, usually reduced to conducting their services clandestinely.

When Emperor Constantine the Great accepted Christianity in 313 A.D., the status of the popes and the Christian community in Rome improved rapidly. From this point on, it was the newly empowered Christians who persecuted the pagans and Jews. The Papacy thereafter became a close partner of the Roman Empire and adapted the administrative structure and similar institutions as the Empire. The cooperative relationship between the Papacy and the Roman Empire, often called *caesaropapism*, lasted until the collapse of the Western Roman Empire at the end of the 5th century. The Eastern Roman Empire, of course, continued for another 900 years from its capital in Constantinople, the modern Istanbul.

Before Constantine's time, the popes had limited influence. Despite Christ's giving St. Peter certain powers over the worldwide Church in the Bible, the early popes were not generally recognized by Christians as supreme much beyond their own jurisdiction in central Italy. After Constantine's time, however, the Roman popes gradually began to acquire more authority throughout, at least, the Western Christian world.

By the beginning of the 6th century, the Western Roman Empire had collapsed under a variety of barbarian assaults, leaving the Pope as the only nominal authority in the city of Rome and its immediate surroundings. He tried his best, with only limited success, to maintain order and authority during this period. Occasionally during these trying years, the Eastern Empire from its capital in Constantinople also attempted to re-establish a foothold in Italy. The most perilous moment, however, was in 451 when Attila the Hun threatened to sack Rome. It was the courageous action of Pope St. Leo I that saved the city. The Pope rode out to meet Attila and informed this ferocious warrior that the wrath of God would be upon him if he entered Rome. Miraculously enough, Attila took the Pope's threat seriously and retreated northward.

Many today feel that Pope Pius XII should have shown similar moral courage in denouncing Hitler and the Nazis, which clearly qualified as one of the greatest violations of Christian values in history. The Vatican seemed to be on a praiseworthy path with Hitler's Germany under Pope Pius XI, who appropriately and courageously issued his encyclical *Mit brennender Sorge* in 1937. This document left no doubt that he considered National Socialism a doctrine not in conformity with Christianity. On his deathbed in 1939 he left the draft of an even stronger encyclical condemning Nazism. Regrettably, Pius XII filed this draft and make no further public declarations condemning Nazi policies.

During the Dark Ages, the authority of the popes as secular rulers of the area around Rome grew. However, as was the case with many medieval rulers, the popes' authority was seriously undercut by the power and belligerence of the local nobility. Significant growth of papal territorial power came in 1115 when Countess Matilda of Tuscany willed her vast tracts of land in North-Central Italy to the Papacy.

From the beginning, the popes were elected by the clergy of Rome. In fact, this practice has persisted until this day, for each cardinal elector is also the parish priest of what is called his titular church in Rome. During several periods, however, the elections were considerably perverted. The worst period in this regard was no doubt during the 10th century when, for sixty years, papal elections, as well as Roman politics in general, were dominated by a mother-daughter team and their various family members. Theodora and her daughter Marozia, two aristocratic Roman women, managed to control several elections, including one that elected Marozia's son as Pope John XI. This period has been nicknamed the Pornocracy, a government by profligate women, as Theodora and Marozia used seduction and murder to achieve their political goals.

By the time of the Renaissance, the papal elections had become more orderly. Yet the cardinals occasionally had difficulty making up their minds. When difficulties arose during the election of 1585, the cardinals decided to try to gain additional time by electing a "stopgap pope." They selected decrepit and stooped-over Cardinal Felice Peretti, who became Pope Sixtus V, feeling confident that he would last only a short time. He upset their plans by living five years and proving to be one of the most vigorous and creative popes in history. When one of his staff

51

asked him how he had managed to become so strong and healthy, he replied that he had always been searching for the keys of St. Peter and now that he had found them he had gained a new lease on life.

With the growth of the merchant classes beginning in Italy in the late 12th century, the volume of wealth in Italy increased exponentially and the revenues to the Papacy increased correspondingly. This was a period of great church building and architectural embellishment in Rome. It was also a period of strong popes and the growth of new religious orders like the Franciscans and the Dominicans. There is no doubt that the moral climate in the Vatican improved measurably during this period.

It is important to bear in mind that with the collapse of the Roman Empire, the population of Rome fell from approximately two million at its height in the 3rd century to around 25,000 by the year 500. Rome was in effect a ghost town. The ruins of literally thousands of Roman buildings lined the streets. Pilgrim guides from as early as the 8th century warn the pilgrim to proceed with great caution through the miles of ruins, often infested with wild animals and robbers, until reaching the safety of the inner walled city. Thus until well into the 19th century, it was never necessary to quarry stone for building in Rome; all the necessary materials were available from the ruins. Most of the earliest churches used columns from Roman temples. A number of medieval churches were actually built inside Roman temples and are still standing today.

As part of his vast urbanization projects in 1586, Pope Sixtus V decided to have the giant Egyptian obelisk moved from the side of St. Peter's Basilica to its current more prominent location in the middle of St. Peter's Square. This was a highly impressive engineering feat for the time. In order not to disturb the workmen involved, the Pope decreed absolute silence, under pain of death, during the entire operation. A famous tale unfolds as follows. As the workmen began hoisting the obelisk, its massive weight stretched the ropes until they were about to break. With panic rapidly spreading among the workers, a voice rang out from the gigantic crowd, "Throw water on the ropes!" The desperate workmen immediately followed this advice, the ropes indeed tightened, and the obelisk was successfully lifted into an upright position. When the man who had shouted out at the risk of death was brought before the Pope, it turned out that he was a sailor named Bresca from the port of Bordighera, a village near Genoa. Overwhelmed with gratitude for his having saved the obelisk, the Pope conferred a papal knighthood on Bresca. He decreed that henceforth all the palms used at the Vatican during Palm Sunday would be supplied by the town of Bordighera, a practice still followed to this day.

The height of papal power came during the Renaissance. At this time, the popes held the balance of power in Italy and commanded large armies and navies. In 1571, Pope Paul V organized the great naval battle of Lepanto, which cracked Ottoman domination of the Mediterranean Sea. Yet the popes' great power and wealth also fuelled considerable corruption. Nepotism was at its height and a newly elected pope normally feathered his family's nest through large grants of papal lands and titles of nobility to his nephews. Many of Italy's greatest families rose to power through the auspices of an uncle who was pope.

Yet during the same period, the popes were also forced to confront the Reformation. As a result, the Catholic Church was significantly reformed during the Council of Trent. Unfortunately, the growing splits in what had been a religiously unified Catholic Church and Europe led to almost 100 years of wars between the various churches and their supporters.

By the time of Napoleon, the Papal States had lost a great deal of their political and military power and the French leader easily overran them at the end of the 18th century. Following the fall of Napoleon, the temporal power of the popes was restored by the victorious powers, those being primarily France and the various Italian states. However, the Papal States were left in a parlous situation with a government that profited but little from the Enlightenment. By the mid-19th century they were among the poorest and most backward territories in Western Europe. Up until 1848, the year of a series of liberal revolutions from Hungary to France, the Papal States proved to be a fertile breeding ground for dissident groups like the Masons and the Carbonari, all aiming to end papal rule.

In 1846 Pius IX was elected Pope, the youngest pope in memory and a declared moderate. Initially, he attempted reforms but when politically motivated violence broke out in Rome, he pulled back. This led to his brief overthrow and the establishment of the short-lived Second Roman Republic. Austrian and French troops put *finis* to this febrile attempt at reform. This sorry state was given the *coup-de-grace* in 1870 when the victorious armies of the new Kingdom of Italy entered Rome. From 1870 to the signing of the Lateran Pact in 1929, the popes were reduced to the status of being only the heads of the Roman Catholic Church, with no pretence of temporal rule as had been the case for the previous more than a thousand years.

V

The Paradigm of a Mini-State

The Vatican City State

The Vatican City State is a sovereign entity, but only in rare instances does the pope choose to act as the head-of-state of the Vatican. The pope normally functions as the head of the Holy See, a perfect sovereignty under international law, as recognized by a great number of countries, especially those countries that have been traditionally Catholic. The concept of the Holy See as a valid entity in international law has frequently proved baffling or unacceptable to the American Government and its international lawyers. In fact, the official definition of the Holy See may appear more appropriate to the realm of metaphysics than to that of political science.

The concept of the Holy See as a perfect sovereign entity grew up centuries ago and is recognized explicitly by all traditionally Catholic states and in practice by any state that maintains diplomatic relations with the pope as head of the universal Catholic Church. In international law, a state is usually defined as an entity that has three essential conditions: a territory, a population, and effective control over the former two. Under the Church's reading of this definition, all Catholics are the people of the Holy See, the territory is made up of those lands over which the Pope exercises "spiritual sovereignty," and the effective control of the

Pope is his control over the spiritual lives of Catholics worldwide. In the view of the Papacy, the Vatican City State merely serves the practical function of assuring that the Church's government is not under the control or influence of a secular state. It must be remembered that during the fifty-nine year period from 1870 to 1929, when the popes had no territory under their authority, they nonetheless managed to maintain their administrative and diplomatic independence from the Kingdom of Italy, all under the rubric of the Holy See.

Foreign diplomats can only be accredited to the Holy See and not to the Vatican. From time to time, the American authorities have tried to get around that point. However, in the eyes of the Holy See, the United States never formally broke diplomatic relations from 1868, when the legation to the Holy See was closed, to 1984, when President Reagan named his friend William Wilson as our first fully accredited ambassador. Once again, I stress that in the eyes of the Holy See, the U.S. never broke diplomatic relations, but simply closed the legation we had maintained in Rome that had been accredited to the papal government. An irrefutable demonstration of the Holy See's position was that throughout the many years during which the United States had no one accredited to the Holy See, the United States was always listed in the *Annuario Pontificio*, the annual directory of the Holy See, as among those countries maintaining diplomatic relations. The names of our representatives were, of course, always left blank.

Vatican Power Structure

At the pinnacle of the Vatican world is the Supreme Pontiff or Pope, who is elected for life by the College of Cardinals. Only those cardinals under the age of 80 are currently allowed to vote in papal elections. However, any cardinal is eligible for election to the papal throne. The pope has numerous roles. Firstly, he is the Bishop of Rome as successor to St. Peter, the first to hold that office. He is also the Vicar of Jesus Christ, the Supreme Pontiff of the Universal Church, the Patriarch of the West, the Primate of

Italy, the Archbishop and Metropolitan of the Province of Rome, and the Sovereign of the Vatican City State.

When a pope dies, limited executive authority is assumed by the Camerlengo of the Holy Roman Church, a position akin to that of a regent. The Camerlengo must be a senior cardinal and is frequently the Cardinal Secretary of State of the late pope. He is, among other things, responsible for the organization of the Conclave that will elect the next pope. The elections are held in the Sistine Chapel and voting continues until one candidate obtains the necessary majority of the votes. Most people are familiar with the famous white smoke that emerges from the stove in the Sistine Chapel, signalling that a new pope has been chosen. Incidentally, the title cardinal derives from the Latin word *cardo*, which means a "hinge," signifying that symbolically the cardinals are the hinges of the Church.

One might think that as an absolute monarch, the pope would be able to rule as he wished. This is far from the case. He is bound by a vast accumulation of rules, dogmas, and traditions going back over a thousand years and if he chooses to depart from any of them, he must provide justification for doing so. In his eyes, he is also answerable to God for his actions and one can easily grasp that this is a strong disincentive against taking rash, revolutionary, or novel stands on important issues. In short, the pope frequently finds himself painted into a corner. This explains the stand of a reasonably liberal pope like Paul VI on the question of birth control. Although he had the strong backing of top theologians for change, he could not justify to himself the possibility of taking the necessary steps. To complicate matters further, popes are older if not old men, who are surrounded by advisors who are also old men. Moreover, they live in a rarefied atmosphere significantly removed from the everyday world and with limited contact with modern ideas. Considering these circumstances, is it surprising that change is not easy to generate?

While I could easily appreciate the difficulty in making changes in the Church in the kind of atmosphere described above, there were times when it was difficult to see why changes that seemed useful and not contrasting with strong theological reasons were so far beyond the grasp of the pope and his inner circle. The birth control issue was a case in point. It is easy to accept that the Church must oppose abortion, but then why also oppose artificial birth control? I was keenly aware that a sizable number of serious and responsible theologians felt that the Church should stick to its well-established position opposing abortion but balance it with a liberalization of its opposition to birth control. Total intransigence on the latter issue seemed unsustainable to these theologians, as with the question of married clergy, and even the whole conundrum of the ordination of women. It is openly admitted in the Vatican that the question of clerical celibacy is merely a tradition of the Western Church and is not a doctrinal matter. The fact that under the umbrella of the pope there are several churches (Ukrainian Uniates, Copts, Maronites, etc.) that do in fact have married priests not only proves the point that the rules of the Catholic Church are not universal, but that the papacy itself can look liberally on the issue. When celibacy was formally instituted in the Middle Ages, one of the strongest reasons behind the move was apparently the desire to stop any thought of clergy leaving church property to their children when they died. The ordination of women is admittedly a harder question, but when one accepts the fact that Christianity is in part a product of the age in which it began, and that having female clergy in the 1st century was obviously unlikely, we can see how the tradition became established. Yet, a lot of water has flowed over the dam in two thousand years and it should not be impossible to update such a matter. Even something as controversial as homosexuality should be viewed in the light of the times when the Bible was written. One could even ask the pointed question of whether the prohibitions on same-sex relations were in the past based on the dire necessity of not doing anything to prejudice the birth rate at a time of high infant mortality, rather than on questions of pure morality. Therefore, even the stand against homosexuality could have originated as a simple device aimed at increasing the population in an age when that was of paramount importance.

Beneath the pope as head-of-state is the Roman Curia or the administrative structure of the Holy See. Directly under the pope is the Cardinal Secretary of State, a position close to that of a prime minister in a civil government. Beneath the Secretary of State is the Sostituto (Substitute), a sort of deputy prime minister, who handles much of the routine work of the Curia, but who, in the case of a weaker Secretary of State, may assume much more authority. During my tenure in Rome, Cardinal Jean Villot, a Frenchman, was Secretary of State. He primarily handled matters of ecclesiastical nature, which permitted the powerful Italian Sostituto, Archbishop Giovanni Benelli, to assume vast powers. This was especially true of matters of an inter-governmental nature; Benelli maintained close and jealously guarded contacts with the diplomats accredited to the Holy See.

The Curia consists of many different offices, mainly of ancient origin, plus a variety of very new ones that deal with contemporary matters like relations with other faiths, population, development, etc. The main offices, or Sacred Congregations, which would correspond to ministries in a civil government, deal primarily with church matters such as the naming of bishops, Catholic education, saints, Church dogma, religious orders, etc.

The diplomatic service of the Holy See consists of clergy from countries all over the world. In principle, any residential bishop may suggest a candidate to study at the Pontifical Ecclesiastical Academy (the Church's diplomatic school) located near the Pantheon in old Rome. The Pontifical Ecclesiastical Academy is the oldest diplomatic school in the world, founded in 1701 by Pope Clement XI. It is a well-known historical fact that the Papacy was in the vanguard in the formation of what later became the universally accepted practices of modern diplomacy. In general it can be said that only highly intelligent and promising candidates are accepted. The successful graduates of the diplomatic school fill the nunciatures and apostolic delegations throughout the world and with time gradually work their way up through the ranks.

A good portion of the staff of the Secretariat of State is chosen from the ranks of the Church's diplomatic service. One can clearly say that the track for advancement to the highest positions in the Church is more often than not through a career as a papal diplomat. This is, of course, not necessarily true of the residential bishops, although many of them may have served in diplomatic capacities. The pool of trained diplomats provides men of well-rounded training who also have impressive skills in dealing in multi-cultural situations, clearly important for today's Catholic Church. The modern Church is truly international and highly respectful of many different cultural traditions.

As the Vatican's pool of experienced diplomats is broadly international in composition and outlook, the dominance that Italians have had for centuries over the top administrative posts in the Church has diminished. Many of my contacts in the Curia believed that Italians were the major obstacle to updating the Church. Although they saw considerable progress underway, they feared that the pace was too slow and continued delay would do great damage to the future welfare of the Church.

Time has shown, however, that Italians were not the only obstacles to change. In spite of his unquestioned personal and political skills, Pope John Paul II did much to turn the clock back to pre-Vatican II times in the areas of theology and Church practices. Pope Benedict also seems unlikely to continue the pace of liberalization and modernization begun by Pope John XXIII and continued so conscientiously under Paul VI. During this more liberal period, the Vatican attempted to fill vacancies in the various national hierarchies with independent, progressive bishops. This was carried out especially in countries where the local governments were weak, or where the Church had a historic image of clericalism and involvement in local politics. In Spain and Latin America, where the Church had such a negative image historically, I witnessed the Church achieve impressive success in changing its perception among the local publics.

With its large residue of conservative prelates left over from the days of Pius XII, the United States was considered by many of my Vatican contacts to be a case apart from the liberalization occurring in other Catholic countries at the time. Due in part to the vast number of American Catholics and the wealth of Catholic institutions in America, the Vatican, to a large measure, left the American Church to run itself. Interestingly, this independence had not provided fertile ground for implementing the reforms of Vatican II, which were often badly presented to the laity by the bishops and priests. American seminaries typically did not recruit a diverse group of men for the priesthood. There was a great deficiency of black priests, which made it very difficult to find qualified black candidates for the hierarchy. The insularity of the Church in the United States was also reflected—or not reflected—in Rome, where American prelates rarely exercised any influence beyond providing funding. European churchmen were far more likely to call on the pope and present him with projects or drafts for what they considered desperately needed reforms. Americans appeared too diffident to take such bold initiatives and hence did not enjoy the degree of influence that their size and wealth could have entitled them to. It must be pointed out that this was a self-imposed limitation and not something imposed on the Americans by Rome.

The Vatican and the American Catholic Church

A conscience goal of the Vatican's was to dilute the historical control over the American Catholic hierarchy by Irish-Americans. With few exceptions, prelates of Irish ancestry had been appointed to most American dioceses since the early 19th century. During my tour, the Vatican realized this goal as Americans of Italian, Polish, Portuguese, and Hispanic origin were raised to archbishop and even to cardinal. In the case of the naming of Humberto Madeiros, a Portuguese-American as Archbishop of Boston, there was a loud outcry of dissatisfaction from the numerous Irish-Americans in his flock.

Despite the lack of approval from the Vatican, some American clergy were active in partisan politics and in electoral office. Rome heartily disapproved of priests serving in Congress. The most controversial was Father Robert Drinan, who represented Massachusetts in Congress from 1971 until 1981, when the Pope insisted he resign. In April 1971, Congressman Bob Wilson of California proposed to Lodge that he appoint Father Martin McManus to our office as an assistant. McManus seemed to have a lot of backers in the Republican Party and their initial goal had been to get the priest appointed as Ambassador to Ireland. Aside from the political inadvisability of having a priest on our staff, his intimate knowledge of the Catholic Church would have been of little use since our mission did not under any circumstances deal with purely ecclesiastical matters. Hence, Lodge wisely denied the Congressman's request.

There was an American at the Vatican who enjoyed internationally recognized standing as perhaps the greatest living Latin scholar. He was Father Reginald Foster, a Carmelite from Milwaukee. The working language of the Holy See is Italian, but the official language is still Latin. This means that the official record copies of all important correspondence and documents must be translated into classical Latin. Reggie was given this heavy and painstaking task. In addition to his normal work, he continued the task of his predecessor, Cardinal Bacci, of creating new words in Latin as necessary, particularly in the areas of sports, informatics, and astronautics. To the delight of many, Reggie adapted the automatic cash machines in the Secretariat of State to work in Latin. This versatile American also conducts guided tours in Latin, does sportscasts, and teaches courses in Latin as though it were any other modern spoken language. His classes are enlivened by the generous use of Latin slang, of which he is a recognized authority. It made me very proud that a countryman of mine had risen to such a rarefied level of scholastic achievement.

Within the Vatican City State

Small as it was, the Vatican City had many attributes and conveniences of any other country. It had a railroad station, radio and television studios, a post office, a bank, a grocery store, a butcher shop, police station, and a dry goods store. The latter store or *economato* was very popular for its high quality and well-priced yard goods and suiting, which were anxiously sought by many clergy. I found that when men dress more or less alike, as the clergy do, differences in quality of fabric and tailoring really stand out. And by this standard there were some very elegant dressers in the Vatican, especially in the Secretariat of State. Since prelates do not wear their formal habits during the normal working day, one has to be aware of how to identify them among the vast throngs of priests and religious. Cardinals usually adorn their black "clergyman" suits with a small piece of scarlet cloth showing at the opening in their dog collar; bishops and archbishops show the same bit of cloth in purple. All three of the foregoing usually also wear a pectoral cross. If they are wearing a cassock, the cardinals have a red sash and a red skullcap; bishops and archbishops have the same in purple. *Monsignore* wear the sash but not the skullcap or cross.

For male clergy there was even a sports club near the beach not far from Rome's Fumicino Airport. There, priests and higher clergy could swim, play tennis or football, or engage in many other sports. I even had one monsignor friend who managed to have himself appointed as chaplain to an exclusive sports club in Rome proper. I sometimes found him there lounging around the swimming pool surrounded by a group of charming young ladies.

All top Vatican officials were not necessarily clergymen. The governor of the Vatican City State was Marchese Giulio Sacchetti, the scion of an ancient Florentine family that had been established in Rome for centuries. The head of the newly created Council of the Laity was Mieceslaw de Habicht, a former Polish diplomat. In addition to the Swiss Guards, most of the other people who lived in the Vatican were laymen and their families. These included some higher functionaries, like lawyers and accountants, as well as clerks and gardeners. Most of the laymen living in the Vatican had Vatican citizenship and carried Vatican passports. Their children, however, were forced to give up Vatican citizenship upon reaching the age of 18, unless they had become formally employed in the Vatican. Almost all the lay employees of the Vatican, except the Swiss Guards, were of Italian origin, and if they lost their Vatican citizenship they automatically reverted to their former nationality, in most cases Italian.

Knowledge of papal heraldry is useful in identifying which pope built almost any structure in the Vatican, or Rome at large, for the popes rarely failed to put their coats-of-arms on anything they had built. Every church, every monument, and even the lintel of every door, had its papal arms. This practice, which is certainly not exclusive to the popes, was started almost with the dawn of heraldry in the late 12th century.

Deep in the bowels of the Apostolic Palaces there were the strangely named *florerie*. These cavernous subterranean warehouses had nothing to do with flowers or any other type of flora, but were vast depositories of a treasure trove of antique furniture, accumulated over God only knows how many centuries. They were presided over by a *floriere* who managed the movement of this storage depot. Vatican offices and senior Church officials resident in Rome had the privilege to borrow items from the florerie to furnish their offices and personal residences. The Vatican probably has the world's largest collection of baroque, marble-top consoles, many of which are still in the vaults. Since clergy assigned to the Vatican normally work long hours, they likely enjoy the possibility of a well-furnished office. Some of the offices I used to visit in the Secretariat of State had glorious furnishings, such as ancient mahogany filing cabinets and large carved desks.

Part of the Vatican City's revenue came from the sale of postage stamps and coins. The designs of these stamps and coins tend to be of very high quality, and in the case of the coins, they are often designed by noted artists that the Popes patronize, like the sculptor Emilio Greco. In addition to normal issues, there are occasional commemorative issues. When a pope passes away, a special issue for the *Sede Vacante* is issued, normally showing the coat-of-arms of the Camerlengo of Holy Roman Church. Entrance fees to the Vatican Museums and other areas also contribute substantially to the income of the Vatican City State.

A sizable area of the Vatican City State is given over to gardens and landscaped areas. Most of the gardens are typically Italian in character, with many formal flowerbeds and numerous Italian stone pines looming overhead. Several grottoes are scattered around these vast gardens, including one dedicated to the Virgin of Lourdes. Among the large number of beautiful fountains my favorite was one with a bronze full-rigged 17th-century war galleon in the middle with water squirting from its cannons. This charming fountain was not always easy to find as it was hidden in a somewhat obscure corner, perhaps to hide its obviously militant character.

In addition to the burial places for the popes in the crypt under St. Peter's Basilica, the Vatican City also has a small outdoor cemetery, the Cimiterio dei Tedesci, or German Cemetery. Perhaps the oldest Christian burial-grounds in Rome, the cemetery was said to have been founded in the early 4th century by Constantine the Great and filled with earth from Calvary in Jerusalem. Pope Pius VI gave it to the Germans in 1779. It can be found just to the left as one enters the Vatican through the Arch of the Bells. The same site also contained a small palace where the popes housed their most distinguished guests during the early Middle Ages. It is said that Charlemagne stayed there when he visited Rome for Christmas in 800, the time when he was crowned by the Pope as the first Holy Roman Emperor, to then rule over great portions of what today is France, the Low Countries, Central Europe, and Germany.

The crypt beneath St. Peter's Basilica contains much of what remains from the first basilica built on the site. The original basilica was constructed under the reign of the first Christian Emperor of Rome, Constantine the Great, in the early 4th century. The crypt now serves as a burial place for the popes, and most of those who have died in the last four centuries have been laid to rest there. In addition to the popes, there are a few royal figures buried in the crypts, including, rather surprisingly to many, four women. Among the royal men are the last three Stuart pretenders to the British throne, The Old Pretender, Bonnie Prince Charlie, and the Cardinal Duke of York. The wife of the Old Pretender is buried there as well. The other three women are Countess Matilda of Tuscany, who in 1077 and 1102 donated a vast tract of land in East-Central Italy to the Papacy that ended up forming a good chunk of the Papal States, Queen Christina of Sweden, who abdicated her throne to become a Roman Catholic, and Catarina Cornaro, Queen of Cyprus.

In 1939, excavations were begun on the ancient Roman necropolis that is just under the crypt of St. Peter's. What is now visible and open to visitors only by special arrangement is a fairly complete cemetery with streets leading between attractive mausoleums. The tops of these mausoleums were cut off when the first basilica was built. They were filled with rubble and the earth levelled to support the new structure. Now, all is pretty much as it had been left in the early 4th century. It was a truly a remarkable experience to walk down the streets of a virtually intact Roman necropolis.

Excavations near the supposed burial place of St. Peter have uncovered numerous ancient coins that show the extensive areas from which medieval pilgrims came to visit the tomb of the Apostle. For instance, there are quite a few Anglo-Saxon coins. This lends credibility to the story from the late 6th century about a visit that Pope St. Gregory the Great made to a public market near St. Peter's, where he came upon a group of blond youths. When he asked a companion who they were, the answer was, *"Angli sunt."* Struck by the fair beauty of the boys, the Pope replied, *"Non Angli sed Angeli."* Following this incident, Gregory became very interested in the state of the Church in England and decided to send Augustine there to be the first Archbishop of Canterbury and to reform the Anglo-Saxon Church.

The Vatican had three levels of tribunals, mainly for the judging of cases in canon law. Criminal proceedings, however, could be brought in a Vatican court, and there was a tiny jail to hold criminals awaiting trial. No long-term incarcerations were made; to the best of my knowledge actual criminals were usually handed over to Italy on the basis of a bilateral agreement.

Given the extraordinary research possibilities available at the Vatican, I obtained passes to both the Vatican Secret Archives and to the Vatican Library. This gave me the opportunity to while away many happy hours of my free time looking up a variety of subjects of interest to me. Monsignor Charles Burns of Scotland, the Assistant Archivist and a noteworthy historian, showed me choice holdings from the archives, which holds impressively complete collections from the 13th century onward and many outstanding documents from even earlier. I used to enjoy the excitement of holding some of these priceless cornerstones of history in my hands. The level of emotion they aroused was palpable.

Initially, this special collection was housed in the Tower of the Winds, the highest point in the Apostolic Palace and the room where the Gregorian calendar was developed toward the end of the 16th century. This rather smallish room had charming frescoes all concerned with astronomical and planetary themes. On the pavement there was also a small version of a meridian, the once popular device on which the movements of the sun could be tracked from a fine beam of light entering through a small hole in the wall. When in 1654 Queen Christina of Sweden abdicated her throne to become a Catholic, she came to Rome and was housed in the Tower of the Winds as an honored guest of the pope. It soon became evident, however, that her life style and open sexual liberality were not compatible with Church standards and she was conveniently moved to another palace just off the top of the Spanish Steps. Incidentally, the archives have a large file dedicated to Christina's tribulations and conversion.

Of particular interest to me in the archives, was the massive file on Henry VIII, which ran from his first request for a divorce from his queen, Catherine of Aragon, to his final excommunication. There is even a letter sent secretly to the Pope by some members of the Privy Council warning that Henry was very serious and was liable to take some drastic action damaging to the Catholic Church in England if no mutually satisfactory solution could be found. More intriguing still was a holograph draft letter which had been misfiled and was found only in 1972. In this letter, Pope Clement VII had in fact made the decision to grant Henry his much desired divorce, but a marginal note advises that under pressure from the lady in question's uncle, Holy Roman Emperor and King of Spain Charles V, the Pope had decided it would not be prudent to approve Henry's wish. I suspect that this significant find was not publicized when I was there because, at the time, Italy was struggling with the question of divorce, and the Vatican surely did not wish to disclose that at any time in their long and troubled history they had looked approvingly on anything connected with the dissolution of a marriage.

Other fascinating documents I studied included a letter of the mid-17th century from the last Ming Empress of China advising the Pope that she had become a Catholic, taken the name of Helena, and had had her children baptized. Needless to say, nothing came of this opening. There were also several golden bulls from the Byzantine Emperors, written in gold ink on purple-dyed vellum. One was a treaty settling (temporarily) the schism between the Eastern and Western Churches at the moment when the Ottoman Turks were threatening the gates of Constantinople. The hand-written notes that Galileo used for his defence arguments during his trial in Rome are there, also numerous grouchy letters of complaint from Michelangelo to the Pope about expenses, payments, and poor workers.

Although I never tried to see it, the Vatican Library reportedly has one of the largest collections of historic pornographic works in existence. The only thing remotely risqué that I did see was a manuscript from about 1100 in the Archives that dealt with reports that the Church in Iceland had lapsed into loose and immoral habits. The scribe, who drafted the manuscript, decorated the margins with salacious drawings of monks and priest carrying off giggling girls on their backs. According to the report, the Vatican had quickly put the Icelandic Church back on the proper track.

The bulk of the files in the Vatican Archives have, in addition to the Vatican's own numbering system, the numbers given to them by the French archivists who were charged with cataloguing them when they were robbed and taken back to France by the Napoleonic Armies. The purloined files were only returned after the conclusion of peace in 1815.

Old buildings like those in the Vatican need constant upkeep by a large team of highly skilled craftsmen. One day I came across a group of workers removing old roof tiles from a wing of the Apostolic Palace, lowering them into carts in the Belvedere Courtyard, which also serves as the Vatican's main parking lot. I curiously asked the foreman when the roof had last been relayed. He said, "Well, you know these things don't last forever." Then he drew out a yellowed piece of paper and looked at it carefully and said, "Oh yes. This was last done in 1787." Now, that's what you call a job well done!

Two things that interest me enormously are history and art, and an assignment to the Vatican was certainly the ideal place to indulge both of these interests. I quickly identified the persons who literally had the keys to the kingdom and made friends with them. Thus armed, I proceeded to ask them little by little to expose their hidden treasures to me. Security and other considerations have by now caused the rules to become tightened, but in my time a more relaxed and laissez-faire attitude prevailed, and I took full advantage of it. In my experience there was a great appreciation on the part of Vatican officials for anyone with a deep interest in their collections.

As every cultured person knows, the Vatican palaces are storehouses of exceptional artistic and historical treasures. Works like Michelangelo's Sistine Chapel paintings are viewed by millions of tourists. Fewer people see the neighboring Pauline Chapel with two of Michelangelo's greatest paintings: the Conversation of St. Paul on the Road to Damascus and the Martyrdom of St. Paul. I had the pleasure of viewing the Sistine Chapel as well as its Pauline neighbor whenever I liked, and this was a singularly exhilarating experience when the former was closed to tourists.

The Raphael Loggias in the Vatican Palace are well known to the discerning traveller, but there are two other great series of Raphael's works that are always inaccessible to the public. One consists of the frescoes in a small porch off the reception-room of the Vatican Foreign Office. These frescoes are all of very pagan grotesques based on paintings that had been discovered during Raphael's lifetime in the Domus Aurea of the Emperor Nero. In this case, grotesque refers to grotto and not to something bizarre. The other Raphael delight is off the Foreign Minister's audience room, a tiny cubicle built for Cardinal Vibbiena as his private bath. These frescoes are somewhat risqué, consisting of cavorting, very fetching nudes!

On one memorable occasion, I was shown the Pope's private Mathilde Chapel on the upper floor of the Apostolic Palace. It was quite small, with a papal throne just to the right of the altar. Right behind the throne in a crystal cylinder on the top of a marble column was a singularly unique relic: the reasonably well-preserved head of St. Lawrence, a Roman soldier who, according to official hagiographies, was roasted alive on a grill in 258 A.D. It is anyone's guess whether these very ancient relics are genuine. Some may well be, but an official in charge of the storehouse of relics from which they are sent out to newly consecrated churches worldwide told me that most relics from before 1200 are open to question. "Just a lot of rubbish," he noted. Notwithstanding, the Vatican possesses many intriguing relics or supposed relics, including the veil of St. Veronica, and the lance that St. Longinus, the Roman centurion, used to pierce the side of Jesus, as well as the head of St. Luke, brought to Rome after the fall of Byzantium in 1453. Sadly, I never managed to see any of these marvels, for even if they might be false they have much antiquarian and historical interest. Following Vatican II, Pope Paul devoted some energy to discrediting a number of famous relics as well as doubtful saints. One victim of this process was the renowned chair of St. Peter in the apse of St. Peter's Basilica, which after careful scientific study turned out to be a 9th century Carolingian throne, probably given to the popes by a son of Charlemagne.

In May 1972, a deranged priest savagely attacked Michelangelo's Pietà in St. Peter's Basilica, a brutal act that caused pain and outrage throughout the world. On May 24 I delivered to Cardinal Villot a very warm letter of regret from President Nixon to the Pope in which he expressed his hope that the masterpiece could be successfully restored. Fortunately, it was. A few days after this tragic event I happened to be visiting the sacristy of St. Peter's, a detached circular building to the left of the main church, where in a small basement room I came upon a table on which the broken fragments of the Pietà had been laid out. I must admit that it was very shocking to see these remnants there, something like seeing a loved one lying dead and abandoned on the street.

Villa Albani in central Rome was built in the mid-18th century and is considered the last of the great Roman villas. Its builder, Cardinal Alessandro Albani, a papal nephew, was an avid collector and a close friend of the father of archaeology, the German scholar Johann Joachim Winckelmann. When Winckelmann was excavating the Emperor Hadrian's villa at Tivoli, the pope naturally had the pick of any treasures found there—and there were an enormous number—but Cardinal Albani had second choice. When I visited Villa Albani, it belonged to Rome's richest man, Prince Alessandro Torlonia, who very kindly opened it for the Lodges and me to visit. The contents are breathtaking. Roman micro-mosaics from Tivoli, the largest collection of pre-classical Greek sculptures outside of Greece, an entire Etruscan tomb of outstanding quality, and much more, all in a magnificent palace without any electricity. Prince Torlonia rarely used the palace, usually only for special family events, and on those occasions the entire building was illuminated with thousands of candles. The spectacle can only be imagined.

The Vatican has control of all the catacombs outside the walls of ancient Rome. What is little known is that there are four ancient Jewish catacombs in Rome. The Vatican jealously guards these Jewish holy sites, much to the consternation of many Jewish religious leaders, who feel it would be more appropriate for some Jewish entity to have control. The Vatican's contention, however, is that only they have the professional and material means to safeguard these priceless relics of Rome's long and distinguished Jewish history. No one knows when or if this long drawn-out battle will be resolved. I regret that I did not try to visit at least one of these Jewish catacombs, which are usually only opened for the occasional scholar.

The four main Christian catacombs in Rome are open all year long, but the other less well-known ones are only open once a year, normally on their patron saint's feast day. A special Vatican body charged with managing all the catacombs, the Collegium Cultorum Martyrum, organizes a mass with processions usually following very ancient liturgies on these occasions. I took part in a few of them, such as the February 14th rites in the Catacomb of St. Valentine. The entire ceremony was conducted in total darkness with only a few candles shedding a minimum of light. As our procession wound its way through the labyrinthine tunnels, it was a moving experience, evocative of the first Christians huddled in fear underground to conduct their prohibited rites.

The Swiss Guards have played a major role in defending the popes since the 14th century, but their status was only put on a formal basis in 1480. The Swiss Guards were traditionally recruited exclusively among German-speaking Swiss Catholics from the canton of Lucerne. By my time, however, due to recruiting difficulties, any Swiss Catholic was eligible. The Guards are normally veterans of the Swiss Army, but on some occasions men have been permitted to satisfy their Swiss military obligations by serving at the Vatican. The colonel in chief was normally a Swiss Army officer, but when I was there he was a lawyer. Only enlisted men use the well-known uniform designed by Michelangelo; officers and sergeants each have their own distinctive uniforms, which are somewhat less colourful. To enter the guardroom of the Swiss Guards is to take a step back into the 16th century. In one section are the most modern automatic weapons, in the other the most ancient ones: pikes, halberds, maces, and two-handed swords. The swearing in of new recruits takes place once a year on May 6th, the day that marks the Guards' heroic defence of Pope Clement VII in 1527 when the imperial forces of Holy Roman Emperor Charles V besieged Rome. This colorful ceremony, complete with a parade, a band playing ancient military marches, and silken banners fluttering in the breeze, takes place in the Cortile di San Damaso, in the heart of the Vatican Palace. After the ceremony, the guests and family members attend a warm and jovial reception in the Guards' ancient barracks.

The Pigna Caffè, located in the Belvedere Courtyard, was a busy gathering place for people working or studying in the Vatican. This tiny café was usually jammed with a loudly chattering group of researchers and staff from the archives and library. The name *pigna* comes from the large bronze pinecone at the entrance that had once stood in front of the first Basilica of St. Peter's, built in the 4th century by the Emperor Constantine the Great, Rome's first Christian ruler.

On the Via Della Conciliazione, the main avenue leading to the Vatican, was the lovely Palazzo Torlonia, built in the 15th century by Bramante. This building had served as the English Embassy to the Holy See until the time of Henry VIII, when relations were broken for well-known reasons. This would make the palace one of the oldest identifiable embassy buildings still standing. The last ambassador, Sir Edward Carne, lies buried at the entrance to the Church of San Gregorio Magno near the Coliseum, a church which still has a British titular cardinal attached to it.

The Alban Hills just outside Rome had been a popular summer address since Roman Imperial times, and the popes were not immune to the charms of this lovely area of lakes and gently rolling hills. During my five years at the Vatican, the Pope took his traditional summer holiday at his villa at Castel Gandolfo. Although his activities were somewhat reduced, he did occasionally conduct a large audience of visitors from the balcony of his villa, which overlooked the small village square. The papal villa, while simpler than the Vatican Palaces, was nonetheless an imposing edifice. It had massive gardens which contained a crypto portico left over from an ancient Roman villa that had formerly occupied the site. There was also a large outdoor swimming pool that Pope Paul never used. At his doctor's orders the Vatican had built a covered cloister on the roof of the Apostolic Palace for Pope Paul to get some greatly needed exercise. Much to the consternation of his staff, he did not use that either.

In the heart of the Apostolic Palace was the office and chapel of the Confraternità della Buona Morte. No longer really an active organization, the purpose of this solemnly-named body had been to assist the moribund to assure that they had a good and spiritually correct passing into the next world. Contrary to what so many modern persons seem to believe, one must remember that in the past it was considered undesirable to have a quick and sudden death. The concept of a good death meant that one would die surrounded by friends and relatives, making memorable last pronouncements. Also essential was the act of bringing anyone into the death chamber that had unresolved bad relations or enmity with the dying person so that a final peace and concord could be arranged.

The last great Vatican ceremony that I witnessed was the opening of the Holy Door in the front of St. Peter's Basilica at midnight on January 1, 1975. Holy years began in 1300 under the pontificate of Boniface VIII and have generally been held every twenty-five years thereafter, although wars and other disturbances have sometimes caused them to be postponed. Just at midnight a fragile Pope Paul struck the masonry door with a silver hammer and slowly the entire door was dismantled and lowered down by a team of masons. In addition to the mortared bricks, the void in the two walls was filled with clean yellow bricks stacked one on top of the other. All these bricks, one of which was later given to me as a souvenir, were placed in the wall in 1950 when the door was closed at the end of the previous Holy Year. They are quite attractive for bricks, each being stamped with the keys of St. Peter and the Roman date for 1950.

One would have hoped that the existence of our mission would have done something to impress upon American officials in Washington the fact that the Vatican City State was not part of the Italian Republic. Unfortunately, we occasionally still received material from Washington and other embassies describing Vatican officials as Italians. For example, a memorandum of conversation between Archbishop Casaroli and Deputy Secretary Rush listed Casaroli as "Italian participant." The worst error, and seemingly the only time it happened at the White House, was a letter from President Nixon to Pope Paul, which was addressed to "His Holiness Paul VI, Vatican City, Italy." In the eyes of my contacts this was assuredly an egregious error.

VI

Pope Paul, the Man and His World

His Holiness Pope Paul VI was in many ways the first modern pope. Elected in the middle of the Vatican Council II, he committed himself wholeheartedly to carrying out the modernizing goals set by that august assembly of the world's bishops. His only reservation on liberal issues, as is sadly known by everyone familiar with subsequent Church events, was his total and immovable resistance to any liberalization of the Church's absolute ban on any form of artificial birth control. The Pope was in many ways more French than Italian in his intellectual formation. A close friend of Jacques Maritain and close to a circle of liberal French cardinals and other clergy, he generally adhered closely to modern ideas conceived in those French intellectual-theological circles.

Pope Paul was frequently called the "Hamlet of the Vatican" due to his public image as a vacillator on pressing issues. Yet in all fairness, this image was mainly derived from his intransigence on birth control, for on other issues he tended to be reasonably decisive. In reality Pope Paul was a very careworn man, who in addition to his age was not too robust. He had a wide circle of friends, many of whom he asked to have intimate meals with him in his private apartment. He particularly enjoyed the company of lay figures in the arts or letters, whom he often had in for a private meal. One he was particularly fond of was Dr. Jonas Salk, whom he never failed to invite to lunch when their two paths crossed. The Pope had an excellent dry sense of humor, and greatly enjoyed the company of young people and even small children. Something else that lighted up his life a bit was to read Agatha Christie detective stories.

I was frequently asked to arrange audiences for Americans, both official and private. In the case of official visitors I often as not accompanied them to see the Pope. Given the frequency of my seeing him over the period of five years I became about as closely acquainted with the Pope as was possible for anyone outside his own world. He was not especially well-preserved for his age, a fact I would suspect was due in part to his lack of good physical exercise. I found him an immensely likeable man whose brilliant intellect and moral power attracted great respect. The Pope always gave some small remembrance to persons he received in private audiences. These were normally rosaries, commemorative medals, or other small tokens. After about a year or so he began to joke with me about how many medals I had accumulated. On a few occasions when he was giving out these medals at the end of an audience he joked that he was running out and would have to ask Mr. Illing to renew his supply. These normally very handsome medals, which were issued each year, came in three flavors: gold, silver, and bronze. The gold were usually reserved for chiefs-of-state, the silver for other high officials, and the bronze for others. On one occasion he splurged and gave Cabot Lodge a gold medal, a highly unusual gesture. He also gave me silver medals on three visits. I felt truly honored indeed.

I never knew whether it was only with persons that he suspected were not Catholics, but in my case Pope Paul always gave me his hand to shake with the palm turned rather upward, seemingly to make it less natural for me to kiss his hand. Given his strongly intellectual bent I sometimes wondered whether he didn't find some of the more ceremonial aspects of his position a bit trying.

His evident pleasure in receiving young people obviously reflected a desire to relax with visitors who did not come into his presence burdened with a massive load of problems and cares. In

January 1973 I accompanied President Nixon's daughter Tricia and her husband Ed Cox to an audience that extended to an unusual 40 minutes. The Coxes were impressed with the Pope's liberality with his time as was I, but the reason was clearly his sheer joy in relaxing with pleasant young guests. He just loved to see a happy, trouble-free young face. He always gave a rousing welcome to the visits of our astronauts and on one memorable occasion a group of White House Fellows. In the latter case he went through the group, asking each fellow which state he was from, and made an apropos comment about each one's home state. We were all totally astounded with his knowledge of American geography.

The Pope was close to his family and was assiduous in performing family baptisms and confirmations, and in entertaining his family on Easter and Christmas in his private apartments in the Vatican Palace. The Belgian wife of one of his nephews, who was a well-known lawyer in Rome, provided me with some charming anecdotes about the Pope at these events. She told me how Pope Paul would organize a lottery to distribute gifts to all the children and would get down on the floor in his white habit and play with trucks and trains, making all the appropriate motor noises to the delight of his relatives, children and adults alike. All the members of the family called the Pope *zio* (uncle) and addressed him with the familiar *tu* form.

Just before my departure in August 1975 I had a 30-minute private farewell audience with Pope Paul. It was a warm and very jolly get-together, unusually long for such a meeting. Pope Paul told me that God had given the United States a most important role in the modern world to make and keep the peace and that we have a sacred trust to fulfil this role. Following his recent meeting with President Ford and his observations of the president in action, he had a definite impression that the president was really taking the reins, especially in foreign policy. He was very gratified about the president's excellent performance to date. We also talked about the European Security Conference, world peace, and the Middle East. In closing the Pope said that, despite its unique non-diplomatic character, he found the Lodge Mission extremely useful to him, and the Holy See greatly profited by having constant contacts and a give-and-take on ideas. When we stood up at the end of this moving meeting I could not help but be struck by the fact that the frail, care-worn old man standing next to me would no longer be a part of my life as he had been for five amazing years.

My farewell audience took place at a moment when Pope Paul was considering whether or not to receive General Mark Clark, who planned to visit Rome shortly. When American troops liberated Rome in 1944 General Clark very wisely made a formal call on Pope Pius XII. During that visit Clark met with then Monsignor Montini, who was at that time serving as Sostituto in the Secretariat of State. From their meeting at such a dramatic moment it was generally assumed that Pope Paul and General Clark were "friends." During our audience the Pope made clear to me that his first meeting with General Clark had not been favorable. He felt that Clark was the man responsible for the bombing of the famous Benedictine Monastery at Monte Cassino and for the subsequent bombing of the Papal Summer Residence at Castel Gandolfo. I pointed out that yes, Clark had been the overall commander of the Allied advance up the Italian peninsula but that to the best of my knowledge, it had been the Anzus sector commander who had actually made the decision on the bombing of Monte Cassino. The Pope then recalled that before our invasion of Italy he had gone over maps of the area with our representative Harold Tittmann, indicating to him the various properties that enjoyed Vatican extraterritoriality. He then asked Tittmann to try to obtain the U.S. Government's agreement to respect these territories when planning the invasion. This request was sadly overlooked. He eventually informed me that he had decided, after long reflection, to see General Clark. He would now see him in peace. He laughed when I said that it would be an act of reconciliation in keeping with the spirit of the Holy Year. Thus ended my five years as the first American representative permanently assigned to deal with the Vatican since World War II.

Pope Paul employed a rather ponderous writing style in his official statements. On several occasions I noted to my Vatican contacts that since it seemed to me that the Pope's objective was to communicate the Church's message to the widest possible audience in simple and clear language, he seemed to be falling short of that goal. In one such address I pointed out that the Pope's opening sentence was long and rambling and contained six, yes six, different punctuation marks. That's true, my friend replied, but then asked, "How many people do you know who can use six punctuation marks correctly in one single sentence?" In the end, it all boiled down to Italian style and the importance of sonority in prose, often at the expense of clarity.

There existed in the halls of the Vatican, especially among the higher echelon, a certain dry and urbane form of humor. The punch lines of stories and witticisms often consisted of apropos phrases in Latin. Since openings for top positions in the Church frequently only became available on the death of an incumbent—something inevitable with so many elderly men occupying the top ranks—one often heard the remark *"Mors tua vita mea."* The practice was also rife in the Church of promoting an incompetent or failed person in order to get rid of him. More often than the Church would like to admit, a cardinal's red hat was rewarded just to get rid of a troublesome or useless prelate. The comment for this was *"Promovere ut removere."* The difficulty of following some of the more rigid Church doctrines, such as the prohibitions of birth control, often drew the observation *"Lex dura sed lex."* These Latin witticisms were endless.

Cardinal Oddi, an old fixture around the Vatican, had gained considerable fame while serving as Papal Nuncio in Brussels with his charming gaffes in the French language. Once, while making an address in Antwerp, he referred to the female mayor as *"la dame publique numéro un de cette ville."* On another occasion, while seated beside a lady whose arms apparently attracted his favorable attention, he said, *"Madame, vous avez des très jolis jambons."*

Pope Paul had a very praiseworthy policy that all members of the Roman Curia should in their spare time engage in some sort of charitable or socially beneficial activity. Even Cardinal Ottaviani, the most conservative relic of the pre-Vatican II Church, had the kindly habit of visiting prisoners at the nearby Regina Coeli

Prison. The heavily overworked Archbishop Casaroli actually lived in a villa donated by a wealthy American lady that served as a halfway house for young men who had been released from detention. Casaroli was extremely dedicated to his charges and frequently took them on excursions into the country or for hikes. In addition to doing good work, the Pope thought that activities that got his staff out of the heavy Vatican atmosphere and into the world at large were very useful. A number of staff members were engaged in teaching at local seminaries and universities.

Paul VI took very seriously the task, set forth by Vatican II, of modernizing the Church. He reorganized much of the Roman Curia and abolished a number of the traditional practices and bodies that had for centuries given a distinct character to life at the Vatican. The Noble Guards and the Papal Gendarmerie were abolished; the use of the *Sedia Gestatoria* (the throne on which the Pope was carried into ceremonies) was significantly limited; Roman nobles lost most of their hereditary functions; and the corps of gentlemen ushers and attendants was greatly modernized. What is little known was the considerable effort Paul VI undertook to physically modernize the general appearance of the Vatican Palaces. The traditional silk damask coverings were removed from the walls of all rooms and were replaced by more cheerful light-colored velvet covering. Hundreds of drawings, paintings, and sculptures by modern artists were acquired and placed on the walls throughout the palaces. This completely enlivened the atmosphere in these formerly sombre buildings. A massive program of modernization was also undertaken in the Vatican Museums, where the crowning achievement was the opening of the Vatican Museum of Modern Art, completely the idea of this pope.

VII

The Vatican Vaults

How the Vatican Acquired its Investment Portfolio

Few subjects arouse more curiosity or wild speculation than the wealth of the Catholic Church and the Vatican. In order to have a better understanding of the Church's wealth, a few essential points must be made clear. Each diocese worldwide is an independent entity for fiscal purposes. Likewise, the Vatican and its administration are separate from the rest of the Church fiscally. Each diocese does, nonetheless, send a small amount of money to the Vatican each year as what has traditionally been called the Peter's Pence. Large amounts are also collected for the charitable and missionary work of the Church and that of the numerous religious orders. Once again, this money does not belong to the Vatican. The next point to make is yes, the Church does indeed own vast amounts of real estate and art treasures in many parts of the world. As often as not, however, this may bring in only relatively limited earnings in the way of entrance fees, as in the case of the Vatican Museums. Moreover, the responsibility of caring for this property often is more of a financial burden than anything else.

The funds which came to make up the Vatican's future investments came into existence at the same time as the Vatican City State under the settlement arranged by Mussolini in 1929. The question of Vatican identity and rights had festered between the Kingdom of Italy and the Holy See since 1870 when troops of the Kingdom of Italy had overrun Rome and put an end to 1,500 years of papal rule over central Italy. From 1870 until 1929, the popes had been virtual prisoners of the Vatican. With the clear object of gaining the sympathy of Italians and also Catholics worldwide, Mussolini had set the goal of reaching a definitive solution of this sore point, the so-called Roman Question. The result was that Italy negotiated and signed three separate agreements with the Vatican: the Vatican Pact that established the Vatican City State as a fully sovereign state independent of Italy; a Concordat or treaty that governed the relationship between Italy and the Holy See in regard to the Church in Italy; a financial agreement making a settlement of all the long-outstanding questions of the seizure of Church property by the Italian Kingdom at the time of the unification of Italy. The amount mutually agreed upon was 750 million lire plus some Italian state bonds. This amount then is the origin of the Vatican's portfolio or liquid wealth.

Vatican "old-timers" had wonderful stories about the negotiations between Cardinal Gasparri and Mussolini. The Italians' initial offers were startlingly generous and exceeded anything the Papacy would have wanted in its wildest dreams. The Italian negotiators first mentioned the possibility of including in the Vatican's territory a respectable chunk of Rome, including much of the Prati neighborhood just east of the Vatican. At one point the Italians even mentioned throwing in Trastevere in its entirety. One usually reliable Vatican source told me that a corridor from St. Peter's to the seacoast near the port of Ostia was also considered. Then it was the Duce's turn to be startled: Pope Pius XI wanted only the barest minimum of territory to guarantee his independence from Italy and to facilitate the Church's carrying out its legitimate business. This ended up being the current Vatican City State around St. Peter's, the pope's summer residence at Castel Gandolfo, and extraterritoriality over a few office buildings and seminaries scattered around Rome. It also included control over all the catacombs under Rome, not excluding the four Jewish ones.

What did the Vatican do with its newly acquired wealth in 1929? By and large, they initially invested it in Italian securities, later expanding the portfolio to other European countries and finally, by the 1960s, into the U.S. market. One of the largest initial blocks was in the Società Immobiliare, also some in the budding Italian airline Alitalia, and the Banco di Roma. The Vatican insisted that a representative of their interests be appointed to the boards of directors. These "Vatican men" enjoyed plum jobs, even in an honest sense, as the pay of board members was often handsome.

One of these Vatican men stands out, if for no other reason than for his name: Prince Pacelli. He was the nephew of Pope Pius XII, the last great nepotist of the Church. Pius revived for his family what had been happily long considered an abandoned practice of naming nephews as hereditary princes of the Vatican. We must remember that as sovereign princes, the popes legally held the right to grant titles of nobility. A short perusal of Italian history leaves no doubt that there were great advantages to be gained from being a papal nephew. The Pacelli family had a history of serving in the papal civil service and over long years had been admitted to the lower or untitled nobility. However, they had yet to become princes. Pius XII saw to it that several of his nephews eventually were placed in top positions in Italian industry. My impression was that with the exception of Pius XII, members of the Pacelli family were not particularly respected in Rome.

Another interesting story of a "Vatican man" concerns the architect Enrico Galeazzi, later named Count by Pope Pius XII, who had been one of the Pope's closest personal friends from the time when the Pope was still a cardinal. How they came to know each other could not have been more amusing. Enrico had a brother, Dr. Riccardo Galeazzi-Lisi, who was an optometrist. As was common in Italy at the time, Dr. Galeazzi-Lisi had a large hanging sign in front of his office, which consisted of two large eyeballs behind a pair of eyeglasses. The story goes that when on one occasion Cardinal Eugenio Pacelli, the future Pius XII, needed the services of a doctor, he recalled the hanging sign and called upon Dr. Riccardo. Although Galeazzi was not a proper MD,

Pacelli liked him and retained him as the papal physician until the end of his reign in 1958. Pacelli became even better friends with Enrico Galeazzi, whom he met through his brother, Dr. Riccardo Galeazzi-Lisi. When Cardinal Pacelli made a memorable trip to the United States, he took Enrico along and introduced him to a string of prominent American Catholics, in particular Cardinal Spellman of New York. As a result of this fortuitous trip to America Enrico was appointed Rome representative of the American Catholic fraternal organization, the Knights of Columbus. But much more important for Enrico was to be named president of the Società Immobiliare, Italy's greatest and most powerful real-estate empire. Here he could look after the Vatican's largest single investment at that time.

Enrico was a delightful and highly cultivated gentleman, who proved highly useful to us in getting established in Rome. When I first met him he was in his 70s and already retired from the Immobiliare. At that time he enjoyed the title "Architect of the Apostolic Palaces," the same title enjoyed by Michelangelo and a string of other eminent architects in the past. Technically, the construction of St. Peter's Basilica has never been declared terminated, and for that reason the workshop or *fabbrica* was still open. The archives of Galeazzi's office were incredible! Complete documentation concerning every detail on the construction of St. Peter's, dating back to at least 1500, including all of Michelangelo's notes and letters from the time when he worked on St. Peter's. It was clear from a rapid perusal of this treasure trove that Michelangelo had been a pretty grouchy individual, who obviously suffered fools badly.

The Vatican's portfolio, all the wealth that had grown out of the initial capital payment received from the Kingdom of Italy in 1929, was administered by the Administration of the Patrimony of the Apostolic See. During my time, Cardinal Jean Villot, the Secretary of State, was the man in charge. He had a team of highly qualified experts who handled the day-by-day work of the office. The office also availed itself of advice from top Catholic laymen in the world of finance and management. This expertise came from all over the world. When I was there, inside estimates placed the full value of this portfolio at approximately $300 million, which was not an excessively large amount for a vast enterprise like the Holy See. By the time I left in 1975, the budget for the operation the Vatican itself was generally considered to be somewhat in the red. The Administration of the Patrimony of the Apostolic See only invested Vatican funds; the Prefecture for the Economic Affairs of the Holy See was charged with preparing the annual budget for the operation of the Vatican and for all the requisite bookkeeping. Cardinal Egidio Vagnozzi, previously Apostolic Delegate in Washington, D.C., was the head of this Prefecture. In 1971 he told us that he had received alarming reports about the future of the U.S. dollar, but that he was replying to all such comments by saying that he was continuing the established Vatican policy of investing in American securities.

The Vatican Bank (IOR)

Last but not least was the Institute for the Works of Religion, the so-called Vatican Bank. Their holdings consisted mainly of the considerable deposits of religious orders and other institutions, plus those of private individuals connected to the Vatican in some way. Some gifts and legacies to the Vatican were also among the bank's holdings. The bank did its own investing, including many Church pension funds, and its earnings were generally at the disposition of the Vatican when needed to fill gaps in the annual operating budgets.

The colourful head of this bank was Bishop Paul Marcinkus, who later become notorious for his involvement in scandals during the reign of Pope John Paul II. Monsignor Marcinkus was a tall, impressive-looking man who hailed from Cicero, Illinois. He had started his career in Rome as a Vatican diplomat, sent from Chicago on the recommendation of Cardinal Mundelein. By the 1960s he was serving in the English Section of the Secretariat of State. Given his impressive size and athletic history, he gradually assumed the additional unofficial task of being the Pope's bodyguard. Marcinkus even stopped a potential assassin who attacked the Pope in the Philippines. Pope Paul clearly liked this engaging American and one day said to him, "Paul, you're an

American and Americans know a lot about business. I'd like to appoint you as head of the Vatican Bank." Paul told me that he was flabbergasted and told the Pope that his knowledge of banking didn't go beyond the monthly balancing of his checking account. Nonetheless, the Pope insisted and Paul got the job.

Marcinkus cut quite a figure in Rome, where his position as the Pope's banker, as well as his golfing skills, made him a sought-after social figure. Needless to say, banks from around the world courted the intriguing figure of the Pope's banker, including the likes of Continental Illinois in the U.S. I remember running into Paul often as the guest-of-honor at fashionable dinner parties in European embassies to the Holy See where the prominent bankers present courted him most assiduously. Bankers, who clearly saw the many advantages that could come from this mysterious, uncontrolled, and virtually unassailable bank, did not ignore the unique character of the Vatican Bank. Money laundering was apparently the objective of some, as subsequent events would show.

By the early 1970s a rising meteor in Italian banking circles was Michele Sindona. In 1974 Sindona, who had become closely involved with the Vatican Bank, fell foul of the law over fraudulent dealings, especially with Wolff Bank in Hamburg. The Italian media accused Marcinkus of making heavy losses with Wolff and assured their readers that he would soon be sent packing. The Vatican press spokesman retorted that the Vatican had managed to lose none of their initial investment, only anticipated interest. I was given the same story and assured that these potential losses amounted to only about $2–4 million. In the end Marcinkus remained at post.

After my departure, Marcinkus and the Vatican Bank became embroiled with another shady Italian banker, Roberto Calvi. Calvi was involved with a number of questionable deals like money laundering, apparently also involving the Mafia. He was found hanged under Blackfriars Bridge in London, no doubt murdered to keep him from testifying. The Italian authorities wanted to question Marcinkus about his and the bank's involvement with Calvi, but the Vatican pleaded sovereign immunity and Marcinkus was dismissed from his position and retired to Phoenix, Arizona, where he died some years later. Had he not become tangled in this web of crime and shady dealings, Marcinkus would surely have become a cardinal. After his fall there was some talk of appointing him as an auxiliary to the Archbishop of Chicago, but all of this came to nought.

To understand the full story of the Vatican Bank scandals, one has to look into just what the Vatican did with some of the money it was earning through its operations, some of which seemed to have been a bit on the shady side. It now seems certain that Pope John Paul II took a very active part in supplying funds clandestinely to the Solidarity movement that was fighting for freedom in his native Poland. It is highly likely that these funds played an important role in strengthening Solidarity and consequently in bringing down the Communist government of Poland. How funds were sent to Poland has never been ascertained. Some speculate that they were moved via Church channels; others allege that the United States played a part. In any case, Polish communism collapsed. It is amazing to think that an elderly Pope may have played as much of a decisive role in triggering the collapse of seemingly monolithic communism as did all the powerful forces in the West.

Henry Cabot Lodge at the North American College with Archbishop Martin O'Connor, Bishop James Hickey, and Cardinal John Wright, July 1970

VIII

Audiences and American Visitors

Papal audiences came in three flavors: general, special, and private. General audiences are massive public affairs, usually held for several thousand visitors in the magnificent modern audience hall; special are small but brief, standing meetings; and private are exclusive and seated, normally in the pope's library/office. The massive effort of handling audience requests for thousands was organized out of the Prefecture of the Pontifical Household. While the head of this august body was a charming French bishop, Monsignor Jacques Martin, the backbone was Monsignor Dino Monduzzi, the hardest working man in the Vatican, bar none. From Romagna, that traditionally anti-clerical area of the former Papal States, Monsignor Monduzzi did his level-headed best to overcome his ancestral heritage. In the office up to seven days a week and working well into the night, he doled out thousands of audience tickets each month and also helped organize all major papal functions, which as one can imagine, were highly-demanding protocol events. The national seminaries in Rome, in our case the North American College, did the actual distribution of general audience tickets. Monduzzi and I worked together constructively—and at times almost conspiratorially—to arrange the two presidential visits that took place on my watch.

While in Rome I was asked to arrange audiences for literally hundreds of American officials or important citizens, ranging from several Apollo astronauts like Michael Collins, to cabinet members like Treasury Secretary John Connally. Connally, who had been ordered by President Nixon to call on the Pope, went very reluctantly to his audience, but when he left he told me that he had had a very important and useful meeting with a surprisingly well-informed man. The wives of American prisoners in Vietnam were frequent visitors, as were a string of senators, especially those wishing to polish up their credentials with the Catholic voters back home.

In early 1973, a large group of prominent Puerto Ricans came to Rome to participate in the ceremonies surrounding the naming of the Archbishop of San Juan, Luis Aponte Martínez, as the first cardinal from our island commonwealth. Due to some confused planning on the part of the new cardinal's staff, Aponte attended neither the North American College's luncheon in honor of the new American cardinals nor the reception at the American Embassy where Ambassador Volpe read President Nixon's warm letter of congratulations. I contacted the new cardinal's secretary to see if I might not be able to put a little balance in matters by offering to read the president's letter, in Spanish if desired, at the ceremony when Aponte took possession of his titular church in Rome. At his request I read him the text on the telephone, which he seemed surprised to find very good. The secretary called me back later to ask if I could attend a dinner after the ceremony of possession and read the president's letter at that time.

At the restaurant I found about 200 animated Puerto Ricans, including many of the island's elite. From my place at the head table I read my own short remarks in Spanish in which I pointed out that San Juan and not Baltimore, as most American Catholics were led to believe, was the oldest diocese in the U.S. and that the cardinal's appointment was a great honor for all Americans, in particular to those who speak Spanish, and as I asserted, will continue to speak Spanish. This remark brought the crowd cheering to its feet. Then I read the president's message, which also deservedly drew shrieks of joy and approbation. At the end of the dinner, I was bombarded with compliments for my speech and told that never had they had a non-Hispanic northerner say such kind and welcome things about Puerto Rico and its people. More of this kind of language would be not only welcome but would help to soothe what was then not the warmest relationship between us all. One cabinet officer told me, "You know, Mr. Illing, the present government in Puerto Rico is not as friendly to Washington as were its predecessors, and your reading of the president's message tonight in Spanish will certainly help to demonstrate to Puerto Ricans that some people up north really care about them."

César Chávez, founder and President of the United Farm Workers Union, had a private audience with Pope Paul on September 25, 1974. The Pope had a high personal regard for Mr. Chávez and had consistently looked with favor on his goals and the methods he used to realize them. In addition to seeing the Pope, Chávez also addressed an unusually well-attended gathering of the heads of Catholic religious orders. He was clearly an undisputed hero of the Catholic leadership in the social and economic areas. A high official of the Justice and Peace Commission told me that without the wholehearted and active support of the local Catholic hierarchy and clergy in California, Chávez's efforts would not have been so successful. The Church considered Chávez a model for the non-violent means of achieving just social objectives. Another top official told me that Chávez frequently wore a Star-of-David around his neck, and when asked why as a Catholic he did so, he replied, "Jesus never wore a cross!"

A low-key but historically significant ceremony took place within the precincts of the Vatican on April 27, 1975, when the Very Reverend Francis B. Sayre, Jr., Dean of the Washington Cathedral, conducted an Anglican Holy Communion service in the oldest church in the Vatican City State, the 5th century Church of St. Stephen, located just behind the apse of St. Peter's Basilica. The Pope had personally authorized this first recorded non-Catholic ceremony to be conducted in the Vatican. Dean Sayre, who was accompanied by a group of deans from North American Episcopalian cathedrals, was the principal celebrant and delivered a magnificent sermon. Although the Vatican Radio carried an interview with Dean Sayre, the Vatican press gave no coverage to this historic event.

When the mayor of my hometown of San Francisco, Joe Alioto, came to Rome in August 1973 to see the Pope, he raised with me afterwards a concern many Mexican-Americans had over the fact that their hero Father Miguel Hidalgo had been excommunicated during the Mexican War for Independence. He wanted to know if anything could be done to rectify that historical problem. I told him, of course, that this was purely an ecclesiastical matter that our mission could not concern itself with, but that I would look into the question just to give him the full picture. I later informed Alioto that my friend Monsignor Charles Burns at the Vatican Archives was certain that there was nothing in the archives concerning Hidalgo, which probably meant that his "excommunication" was not official, but was very likely just a local lifting of his right to exercise priestly functions. To get to the bottom of the story, Burns suggested that the mayor have research undertaken in Mexico, where the records most likely resided.

One of the more intriguing Americans to show up at the Vatican during my stay was Dr. Gianni Dotto, an inventor holding a considerable number of patents connected with the automobile industry. Dotto came to Rome with his Dotto Ring Device, an amazing contraption based on his concept of thermal-magnetism. The theory was that if you heat one pole of an electromagnet and greatly cool the opposite pole, you will accelerate the movement of the magnetic field. Dotto was convinced that this type of thermal-magnetism was beneficial in curing many illnesses from mental disease to cancer. His belief was that many such disorders were caused by morbid misalignments of the DNA, a problem that in many cases he asserted his Dotto Ring could correct. The embassy's scientific attaché also spoke to Dotto and found him to be a serious scientist and definitely not a quack. However, he could make no judgment on the utility of the ring device for rejuvenation or for the cure of certain disorders.

I met Dr. Dotto through the private secretary of Cardinal Amleto Cicognani, the former Secretary of State, who was in his 90s and lived in a grand apartment near the Pope in the Vatican

Palace. Dotto admitted to me that he had gained access to the Vatican through the good offices of ex-King Umberto of Italy, and that he had installed one of his ring devices in a small room in Cardinal Cicognani's apartment. The device had been leased to the Cardinal for an 18-month period at a nominal fee. Dotto showed me a lease contract of unquestionable authenticity signed and sealed by Cardinal Cicognani. He also showed me photographs, which he admitted taking clandestinely, showing what could easily have been Cardinal Cicognani's apartment and the room with the device. Dotto also claimed to be working closely with the Pope's private physician, Dr. Loris Fortuna, in administering his treatment to both Pope Paul and Cardinal Cicognani.

Shortly after I met Dotto, the famous Hollywood star Gloria Swanson showed up at my office. She expressed the strongest conviction that Dotto was "the real article" and that he had achieved great success in curing many illnesses. Shortly thereafter, Dotto managed to get the support of some religious orders, open a luxury clinic off the Appian Way, and begin receiving patients. I visited the clinic a few times, and during one visit, the head nurse-nun told me of a man who had arrived by private plane on a stretcher, supposedly in the last stages of advanced cancer. Within a few weeks, she swore that he had walked out greatly improved. Then, all of a sudden, the clinic and the entire operation rather mysteriously disappeared from Rome. Visiting with Gloria Swanson was delightful. She was a truly fascinating character, full of interesting stories about her long life and deeply into pyramidology and other occult beliefs.

I recently searched Dotto on the internet and found that he had died at his home in Italy, according to some accounts the victim of a brutal murder in which he was run over by car many times. He is listed among many other scientists on some web sites as one of many energy researchers whose work had been suppressed by large energy companies to keep their efficient discoveries from competing with their industries. Like Dotto, others had been murdered, according to these conspiracy mongers. Drug companies had also been involved in suppressing some discoveries. In Dotto's case, it is even asserted that cancer institutes like

Sloan-Kettering in New York had helped to suppress his successes in treating cancer with his ring device. And so, Dotto lives on in conspiracy circles!

Pope Paul with a group of Canadian Indians

IX

The Diplomatic Whirl

The Nature of Diplomacy at the Vatican

Diplomatic life in Rome operates in something of a maze, given that there are in reality three separate sets of diplomatic missions, as well as a fourth category which sweeps up a number of disparate entities. The first group is made up of the diplomats accredited to the Italian Republic; the second group includes those accredited to the Holy See; and the third group includes those accredited to international organizations, primarily to the United Nations Food and Agriculture Organization (FAO). The fourth group consists mainly of cardinals either working in the *Curia Romana* or resident in Rome, and at my time also included the exiled kings of Greece and Afghanistan. Each of these diplomatic groupings had its own designated automobile license: CD-1, CD-2, CD-3, and CD-4.

As though these four groupings did not provide enough complication, the situation was complicated even further by the existence of missions accredited to the Sovereign Military Order of Malta, more commonly know as the Knights of Malta. Headquartered in Rome since the Napoleonic seizure of their sovereign bastion on the island of Malta, the Knights of Malta enjoy sovereign status under international law. In most cases, those countries having diplomatic ties with the Order of Malta had a dual accreditation with the Holy See. The knights themselves had an interesting representative to the Vatican, the venerable Count Stanislao Pecci, a nephew of Pope Leo XIII, who had died in 1903.

My arrival produced something of a diplomatic puzzlement; I was working exclusively with the Vatican but not accredited, yet given courtesy diplomatic status by the Italian Government, which handled all the housekeeping details for the diplomats accredited to the Holy See. After a lot of heavy pondering, it was decided that I should be given CD-4 license plates for my private vehicle. This immediately catapulted me into a rather rarefied and exclusive company as described above. The prestigious nature of my new outward status was made clear by the way the Roman traffic police treated me. They clearly could not have taken me—or my wife—for a cardinal, but I suspect that they may have supposed that I was some sort of rather obscure royal personage, who was somehow worthy of their respect. In any case, it was an unexpectedly enjoyable privilege to be waved through intersections and ushered into parking places.

It was a not always a rigidly observed practice to maintain a scrupulous separation among the various diplomatic groupings in Rome. The separation was, however, strict for official functions. On the more informal social level, one could, without criticism, on occasion mix closer friends from the one corps with people both from the Vatican bureaucracy itself and diplomats accredited to the Holy See. There was a fair dose of snobbism among diplomats accredited to the Holy See; they definitely considered themselves somewhat superior to their colleagues dealing with Italy.

The diplomatic and official atmosphere at the Vatican was not unlike what must have existed in a smallish royal court in the 19th century. After all, the Papacy is pretty much an absolute monarchy. During my time Pope Paul was something like an aged widower prince, who only did the absolutely necessary types of official entertainments, something like the Emperor Franz Josef in his last years. In the case of the Vatican, that consisted almost exclusively of inviting the local diplomats to religious ceremonies and to the occasional reception or lecture. On the other hand, the various missions themselves engaged in the normal round of diplomatic entertainments.

Great Vatican Ceremonies

Functions at the Vatican were very formal. Normal dress at the great ceremonies in St. Peter's Basilica and the other great churches in Rome was either diplomatic uniform or white tie with black waistcoat for the men and long, black dresses with the head covered for the women. Decorations were *de rigueur* on these great occasions. There were four large tribunes, or boxes, set up at the bases of the four gigantic pillars around the high altar of St. Peter's. One of these, the Tribune of St. Veronica, was reserved exclusively for the diplomatic corps. Just opposite, was the Tribune of St. Longinus, where other distinguished guests were seated. That was my spot, usually in the front row, a privilege I certainly would not have been accorded had I been a properly accredited diplomat. I was also expected only to wear a normal dark suit on all these occasions. Incidentally, the chapel high above where the diplomats sat contained the veil of St. Veronica and the one above where I sat contained the lance that St. Longinus had used to pierce the side of Jesus at the Crucifixion. In spite of repeated requests, I never managed to see these two startling relics.

During my tenure, in addition to the great ceremonies at Holy Week and Christmas, there was the occasional canonization or beatification. From time to time there was also the solemn and austere funeral of a cardinal. A cardinal's coffin is simply laid on the floor with no flowers. Perhaps this simplicity is to compensate for the splendor a cardinal often enjoys in life. I found the Maundy Thursday rites particularly touching. The pope walked passed a group of twelve males to wash each one's feet in imitation of Christ's gesture at the Last Supper. I especially remember this very moving and emotional ceremony one year when the participants were men from a modest old people's home. The Christmas Eve mass in the Sistine Chapel was also very grand with Michelangelo's ceiling and front wall all aglow in the blazing candlelight. Diplomats were usually permitted to have their children receive their First Communion directly from the pope on that evening.

At the close of one great Maundy Thursday ceremony in St. Peter's, an embarrassment occurred involving our little mission. As was the norm, 50 or so young priests dispersed throughout the Basilica to distribute Holy Communion. A tall, dark, red-haired young priest, possibly an American, approached the tribune of St. Longinus where I was seated in the first row next to Ambassador and Mrs. Lodge. Close members of the Pope's family were seated next to us. Normally on these occasions, the priest did not approach you unless you gave some sign that you wished to take communion. This priest, however, seemed to be convinced that everyone would naturally accept the sacrament, although he certainly was not insistent. When he stood before me I shook my head slightly and he moved on to Mrs. Lodge, who made a similar negative sign. When Ambassador Lodge saw the priest's friendly presence he accepted the proffered communion wafer with a smile.

On the way back to the hotel, Mrs. Lodge and I questioned the ambassador about taking communion, fearing that some Catholics might take umbrage at a non-Catholic participating in their sacrament. Lodge said he felt that we must be ecumenical and that he personally felt very ecumenical and brotherly toward all fellow-Christians; therefore, he saw nothing amiss in having taken communion. Seeing the priest before him, making the offer, it seemed the most natural thing in the world to accept. Besides, he said, he suspected that his friend Cardinal John Wright had put the priest up to it.

After we took our seats in St. Peter's Basilica the following day, Commendatore Giovannini, the chief papal usher, called me aside to ask if, on the previous day, the priest had forced Ambassador Lodge to accept communion. I told Giovannini that I was not aware of the details but assured him that the priest exercised not one bit of pressure on Mrs. Lodge or myself, and that, moreover, the ambassador was very ecumenical. Once again, Giovannini insisted that it was very important to know whether the priest had importuned Lodge or not. I stressed that I seriously doubted that coercion of any degree was involved and assured him that the Ambassador was not in the least displeased or even mystified. I trusted that my efforts may have dispelled any intention there may have been to discipline an erring but assuredly well-meaning young priest.

As a mid-level diplomat, I would not have enjoyed the kind of reception I was almost automatically given both by the Church officialdom and by members of the diplomatic corps accredited to the Holy See. This was, of course, not due to my great charm or overwhelming brilliance but to the obvious fact that I was the only representative available from the great American super-power. As Ambassador Lodge normally only spent about four weeks a year in Rome, I was, for all practical purposes, the de facto *chargé d'affaires*, but of course not officially. My position was what in diplomatic parlance would be designated as "officious." In any event, I was generally treated as a chief-of-mission by the accredited ambassadors and was dealt with on an official and social basis accordingly.

One of the very useful and somewhat novel practices at the Vatican was the open house for official callers that the *Sostituto* (the "deputy prime minister" in the *Curia Romana*) held every Thursday morning in his office. There were no appointments and everyone who attended was received on a first come, first served basis. When entering the small waiting room you usually found a number of persons before you. They could be ambassadors, cardinals, bishops, or other ranking officials of the church. It often turned out that the conversations one had in the waiting room were as interesting and useful as the ones one eventually had with the *Sostituto*, at that time Archbishop Giovanni Benelli. On one occasion in 1971, I came upon a gentleman whom I quickly recognized as Cardinal Wojtyla of Krakow, the future Pope John Paul II. I recall finding him an extremely affable man with a delightful sense of humor. We managed to have an engaging conversation alone for over an hour while we both patiently waited our turns. He told me that he felt that the new political climate in Poland hopefully presented certain opportunities for the Church to improve its position. He noted, however, that the Soviet Union was suspicious of an international religion like Catholicism—a heritage from czarist times—and would urge its satellites to proceed cautiously when dealing with the Vatican. Wojtyla also described in glowing terms his tour to Canada and side visit to the United States. One of his reasons for being in Rome was to brief Vatican officials on Polish Primate Cardinal Wyszynski's latest talks with Polish leaders.

High Quality of Diplomats at the Vatican

What could be more painful for a Cuban ambassador than to be hoodwinked into getting friendly with an American diplomat? That is just what happened in Archbishop Benelli's famous waiting room. Luis Amado Blanco, a rather renowned poet, was Cuba's sitting ambassador to the Holy See as well as dean of the diplomatic corps. He was an old-line socialist with a reasonably warm feeling toward the Church; his wife, moreover, was a practicing Catholic. When I first saw him in the waiting room, I immediately realized who he was. Since my Spanish is quite good, and with a distinctly Iberian accent, I decided to go up and engage him in conversation. As the waits were often somewhat lengthy, we managed to have an extended and very agreeable chat about Vatican matters. I made sure, however that we did not touch on Cuba or the U.S. At the end, he asked me where I was from. I said America, at which he asked, "Yes, but which country?" To my answer of the U.S., he was at first rather taken aback. Nonetheless, our subsequent meetings were always invariably pleasant, even when he had the misfortune of being accompanied by one of the obvious thug-types from his embassy. Our last meeting was at a lecture at the English College. He was particularly warm and friendly that evening and we talked like old chums about people in the Vatican and even my Cuban ancestors. The following morning, the morning of March 9, 1975, he died suddenly from a heart attack. Quite poignantly, I must have been the last person to have a serious conversation with him.

In general, the ambassadors sent to the Vatican, especially those sent by Catholic countries, were of a high caliber. When not highly regarded senior diplomats, they were often prominent figures from the world of letters or scholarship. France in particular had a list of outstanding representatives, including René de Chateaubriand in the early 19th century and Jacques Maritain and Vladimir d'Ormaisson in the 20th.

Among the diplomatic novelties at the Vatican were representatives of the Lithuanian and Polish governments in exile. Nationalist China also had a delightful presence in Ambassador Chen Chihmai and his lovely wife Lilyan. One European ambassador was Jewish and two others were gay. The first country to name a female ambassador was, to my knowledge, Uganda. Non-Catholic countries like Great Britain and Finland usually had a non-Catholic chief-of-mission and a Catholic deputy chief-of-mission. The charming Iranian ambassador, Mehdi Vakil, who was close to the Shah, had the pleasant additional task of purchasing valuable works of modern art for Iran's Museum of Modern Art. The walls of his apartment formed a revolving gallery of glorious paintings. The Turkish ambassador, a wonderful and highly cultured man whom I had the pleasure to have known in Belgrade, had the monstrously bad fortune to be assassinated on his doorstep in Rome by Armenian terrorists.

My attempts at entertaining in my home were, by necessity, fairly simple, although I did from time to time have a cardinal for a dinner-party. The great embassies, on the other hand, really pulled out all the stops with their receptions. It was expected, for example, that each embassy would have a small drawing room reserved exclusively for cardinals, who might wish to withdraw if even for a short time from the clamor of a reception. No one else was expected to enter these especially reserved rooms except when summoned by one of the cardinals inside. Another special touch was that on arrival, cardinals were to be met at their vehicles by two lackeys bearing lighted torches, and then escorted to the head of the receiving line.

Due to his illustrious reputation and connections, Lodge was authorized to use a representation allowance that, for the parsimonious State Department, was quite substantial. He did most of his entertaining at the fashionable Grand Hotel, usually in one of the elegant private dining rooms. He rarely invited more that ten guests, mixing some old friends with Vatican officials and diplomats accredited to the Holy See. To gather material for the reports we sent back to Washington we often relied upon one-on-one affairs, usually lunches at local restaurants. On several occasions, we were invited for meals at monasteries where the atmosphere was not unlike that of a more intellectual gentlemen's club. Since Lodge was normally not in Rome for more than five weeks a year, he generously let me use the bulk of his allowance. The result was that I had a representation allowance exceeded only by that of our Ambassador to Italy. I was never sure that this was not something of a sore point with my colleagues at the embassy.

During my assignment, I never knew Pope Paul VI to go out socially. In the past, the Pope's predecessors often did, mainly during the time before 1870 when the Papal States were a proper country. The last pope to be entertained widely was Pius IX. He frequently dined at religious houses and the great princely palaces of Rome. When he dined, a small, detached table was set for him, just next to the main dining table. His small terrier frequently accompanied him. Pius IX also loved a good cigar after meals. Each Roman prince had a throne-room in his palace where the pope could sit when being entertained. When the Italians seized Rome and put *finis* to the Papal States in 1870, the great Roman families turned these thrones to the wall as a gesture of protest. To this day, some of these thrones are still symbolically turned to the wall. Another princely protest was to seal the main street door of the palace as a sign of extended mourning for the demise of the Papal States. In 1970, I witnessed Prince Lancellotti open his street door for the first time after it had remained closed for exactly 100 years. After all, a protest can last only so long!

Some of the embassies to the Holy See enjoy truly magnificent establishments. The Italians have a lovely, small palace built by the Medici Pope Pius IV on via Flaminia. The French Villa Paulina was built for Napoleon's sister Pauline, who was married to the Roman Prince Camillo Borghese. The Portuguese have a glorious villa in the Parioli district, and, of course, Spain has a palace on the *Piazza di Spagna*. The Spanish Embassy is the longest established diplomatic mission in the same building in the world, in use since the early 17th century.

In addition to the splendid premises, the Spanish Embassy had another rather special quality: its own resident ghost, Padre Piccolo. This Capuchin father was a confessor in the neighborhood of the *Piazza di Spagna* in the early 17th century. He was reportedly carrying on a love affair with a lady who lived in an apartment in what is now a wing of the embassy. Surprised one day *in flagrante*, the lady's irate husband threw the priest down the stairwell to his death. A rather life-like specter, he frequently haunts this stairwell and has been known to give polite directions to visitors to the embassy staff apartments. Guests arriving at parties are indeed startled to learn that the kindly priest who directed them to the right door has been dead for almost 400 years!

President Nixon certainly had his shortcomings, but ignorance of foreign policy and diplomatic niceties was not one of them. He no doubt wanted to please American Catholics by sending a representative to the Vatican. At the same time, Nixon wished to make clear that the reasons for having representation in Rome were purely practical and political and in no way involved religious matters. To emphasize that point, he scrupulously avoided any temptation to send a Catholic. He did not wish to give the impression that a desire to impress Catholic voters entered into his calculations.

American Catholic Diplomats at the Vatican

From my perspective, and much to their credit, American Catholics seemed less blasé about their religion than many "Old World Catholics," who seemed affiliated to their religion for almost historical-sociological reasons. I personally remember a rather embarrassing audience with the former mayor of a great Eastern American city who went on *ad infinitum* about his great loyalty to the Church. The Pope was visibly uncomfortable and not used to such showy displays of religious zeal. The typical European diplomat or official would have assumed that the Vatican took his Catholicism for granted and acted accordingly.

Genuflecting and kissing the papal ring are normal practices for any Catholic meeting the pope, but are generally avoided by top-ranking European officials and ambassadors. The principle is that one is calling on the pope as the representative of one sovereign state to another sovereign figure. When an American official calls on the pope, he does so as the representative of the President of the United States, not as a member of any particular religion. Ring kissing is totally inappropriate for any high American official calling on the pope, and is generally viewed by non-Catholics as offensive.

John Volpe was American Ambassador in Rome during my last two years there. A singularly impressive self-made man, Volpe had been Governor of Massachusetts and the United States' first Secretary of Transportation before his assignment to Rome. Yet Volpe had his critics. Nixon told Lodge that he found Volpe an insufferable chatterbox who took excessive time during cabinet meetings talking about his department. Additionally, many complained that a sacred State Department rule against sending an Italian-American to Rome had been broken by naming Volpe to Italy. Volpe really had wanted the job at the Vatican, but Lodge was already there. For many years, Volpe had been cultivating Italian politicians as well as visiting his family's ancestral village in the Abruzzi region east of Rome. The mayor of the village went along with the rather demanding festivities expected each time Volpe visited but he let the embassy know that it was somewhat expensive for his small village to entertain the native-son who made it big in America.

While Volpe had no official contacts or duties with the Vatican, he did endeavor to spend time in Vatican circles in his capacity as a Catholic layman. During one Easter Week ceremony at St. Peter's, Ambassador Volpe was seated next to two French women. At the end of the ceremony, since President Pompidou had just passed away, Volpe very courteously offered his condolences to them. One of them replied somewhat haughtily that in her family there is no President of France. The next day Volpe asked me who the woman was who made such a peculiar remark.

I informed him that she was the wife of the Bourbon pretender to the French throne.

During my years at the Vatican, I acquired some expertise on orders of knighthood, and on bogus orders of knighthood in particular. It was not uncommon for some down-at-the-heels European nobleman to resurrect a long defunct order of chivalry, and then to offer its decoration free to unsuspecting ambassadors and other prominent persons. Once the "revived" order had a small stable of prominent members, the nobleman began to sell the decoration to less glamorous candidates. All of our ambassadors at Rome received such offers. Ambassador Volpe came to me from time to time for advice. I invariably pointed out that the offers were not legitimate and were to be avoided like the plague. On one occasion, however, he was tempted and accepted a marginally fake order connected with a branch of the Orthodox Church in the Middle East. It was a very attractive decoration, as they usually were!

Novel Contacts in the Vatican World

In a typically subdued social atmosphere like the Vatican diplomatic world, it was from time to time a pleasant surprise to come across something different or even startling. I remember one such pleasant surprise in 1969 when I visited the orthodox monastic enclave of Mount Athos in Northern Greece, a territory where all female creatures are excluded, except of course for birds. Totally out of place but basking in her maternal splendor was a mother cat, nursing her litter. How—and why—the monks permitted her to be openly there was a mystery.

The pleasantly startling anachronism at Vatican receptions was the Contessa Ghezzi, an eighty-something-year-old widow of a prominent Vatican lawyer. The Countess frequently appeared in a modified bull-fighter's attire complete with trousers and a jacket covered with glistening sequins. She selected vibrant colors from bright orange to green, which complemented her flaming red hair. Despite her rather flamboyant appearance she was a lady of flawless dignity and propriety. She usually gave one smallish reception a year at her apartment, during which she followed what she claimed was a long-lost custom of aristocratic Roman ladies to display their handiwork with a needle, which in her case included quite frilly under-garments. These were all carefully laid out in her bedroom for all the guests to admire.

Recently in the news, we have seen Muslims outraged over cartoons published in Denmark showing the Prophet Mohammed in disrespectful circumstances. Strangely, the Danes were involved in a similar controversy in 1973 due to plans to produce a film on the love life of Jesus. The non-resident Finnish Ambassador to the Holy See, Jussi Mäkinen, told me how this situation led to his greatly increased standing with the Pope. When the ambassador saw the Pope in November 1973, the Pope asked if Finland, the only Scandinavian country having diplomatic relations with the Holy See, could use its influence with the Danish Government to halt the film. The ambassador passed the request on to Helsinki and by late November, the Danish Government had withdrawn financial support to the filmmaker. The apparent reason was that the producers were unable to find a country in which to make the film by their deadline. Regardless of the real reasons, Mäkinen said, the Pope had chosen to credit Finland with the success and had been treating Mäkinen accordingly.

An amusing friend of the Lodges in Rome was a very elderly Russian exile, Betty Buzzard. Born Elizabetha Hoyningen-Heune and considered one of the greatest beauties of the pre-Revolutionary Russian Court, Betty became acquainted with the Lodges during their 1923 honeymoon in Paris when they visited her *haute couturier* shop on the Place Vendôme. By 1970, she was the widow of the late Major Buzzard, a Briton. Her tiny apartment was a center of social life for the Russian émigré community, but her delight was to entertain young people. From time to time she had the Lodges or me over for dinner. When she died in her 90s, Lodge and I attended the powerfully moving Russian Orthodox funeral, after which we left the cemetery prostrate with emotional exhaustion.

There were two extraordinary American women living in Rome of whom I have colourful memories. The Marchesa de

Chiusi was the last living descendent of Betsy Ross, who sewed the first American flag for General Washington. She lived in the Palazzo Taverna on a modest pension that a wealthy American lady had granted her upon learning that an American of such distinguished ancestry was penniless. The other was Mrs. Bloodgood, also resident in Palazzo Taverna. She, like la Chiusi, had spent the entire war in Rome, and when the Italian police occasionally visited her apartment to advise her that she was an enemy alien and should leave Italy at once, she drove them off in a rage with phrases like, "I don't care a hill of beans about the war or your silly *Duce*. Go away and leave me alone." Being of formidable appearance, she managed during all the war years to make her point.

President Ford departing Rome after a call on the Pope

X

Welcome to the Vatican, Mr. President

Without any doubt, the most onerous chore any embassy can be called upon to perform is to organize a presidential visit. The often dissimilar protocol styles and customs of two governments have to be harmonized and numerous rough edges must be smoothed, a process that is often still going on after the visit has begun. Last minute changes are frequently imposed after the embassy had believed that everything was finalized and something is sure to go wrong no matter how hard both parties have tried to organize things to perfection. There are in reality three rather than two parties involved in arranging a presidential visit: the host country, the White House, and the embassy. The embassy is as often as not caught in the middle, although it is clearly tasked with defending its country's interests.

Just four months after my arrival in Rome, we were advised that President Nixon would be making an official visit to Italy and to the Vatican to call on the Pope on September 28, 1970. It was established practice that any American president visiting Italy would also call on the pope. Likewise, an American president visiting the Vatican was expected to call on the Italian Embassy. Unaware of this protocol, President Lyndon Johnson once stated his intention to call on the pope but not on the Italians as he felt this too time-consuming and not necessary on that particular stop in Rome. When Ambassador Frederick Reinhardt informed

Johnson that such a thing just could not be done, the President restated his refusal to visit the Italian Embassy. Rather than accept that he had fulfilled his professional obligation to advise the president, Reinhardt continued to object strongly. In the end, Johnson relented, but on his return to Washington he obtained the ambassador's head. Thus, for an excess of zeal, ended an otherwise brilliant diplomatic career.

One can easily imagine that the prospect of organizing a presidential call on the Pope with our staff of two appeared rather daunting. We, of course, had the embassy at our disposal for many logistical matters as well as the typically overbearing and demanding White House advance team, complete with the Secret Service people. Even though the President's visit to the Vatican would be for no more than two hours duration, everything had to be planned to the minute detail. Normally, members of the advance team accompany embassy staff to discuss details with the host country. This was not the case for us, however, as the Vatican wished only to deal with the Lodge mission regarding arrangements for the presidential visit. Although flattered by this display of faith in our little mission, we were overwhelmed at times by the panic-inspiring task ahead.

To avoid chaos and confusion with the advance team from Washington, I had to quickly establish my unequivocal authority in all contacts with the Vatican to make it clear to them that the level of security within Vatican City was of the highest order, and to make sure they understood that when Vatican officials said no on a particular request the answer was likely to remain no. After over one thousand years of receiving chiefs of state by the popes, the Vatican undoubtedly knew the ropes. I must say that with firmness and politeness I managed to convince the advance teams that I knew of what I spoke and that I would advocate their interests as firmly and successfully as possible.

One of the thorniest requests was that Secret Service agents could ride on the running boards of the security car that rode in the motorcade just behind the President's limousine. Despite repeated requests the Vatican refused to budge on this. In the end, the American side agreed that there would be no agents on the running boards. But lo and behold, when the motorcade entered Vatican territory though the Arch of the Bells just to the left of St. Peter's—there were four armed agents riding on the running boards! At this moment a group of plainclothes Vatican police ran out and tackled the Secret Service agents and pulled them to the ground. We were all horrified to see them wrestling furiously on the ground. During this terrifying and unheard of altercation, the motorcade had slowed down to a snail's pace— something totally unexpected and potentially frightening. Obviously surprised, Nixon asked Lodge what was happening, and Lodge, who could see back from the jump-seat where he was, said, "Oh, just the usual antics of the Secret Service." Nixon replied, "Those guys never know when to stop!" Order was rapidly restored and we moved on to the scheduled meeting with the Pope.

After entering the Vatican City through the Arch of the Bells, Nixon's party was greeted by a number of English-speaking Gentlemen of His Holiness, distinguished laymen who serve as chamberlains or ushers for papal protocol events. Then up the elevators to begin a rather long, winding walk through the beautiful halls of the Palace into a rather small waiting room complete with a painting of St. Peter by El Greco. Just before arriving at the waiting room one passes through a small throne room where the Pope usually receives new ambassadors. From the waiting room, the persons to be received by His Holiness are led into his office/library. The office is of medium size and is simply furnished but with a number of priceless paintings on the wall.

In the anteroom, just before going into the private audience, I had the chance to meet Nixon and exchange a few pleasantries with him. Observing him for about 20 minutes I got the impression of a man not totally at ease with himself. This was certainly not a question of not knowing what he was doing or of how to handle himself, but rather of someone not especially comfortable in his own skin. His insecurity was palpable, and I doubt if it had anything whatsoever to do with being in the Vatican. Despite having achieved as much as any human being possibly could, Nixon was simply a psychologically insecure man.

My next presidential visit was on June 3, 1975, near the end of my five-year tour. This time it was the much more affable and relaxed Jerry Ford. Arrangements went smoothly, the White House people seemed less haughty, and the only uncomfortable Vatican demand was that Secretary of Defense Melvin Laird not attend the audience. This was at the termination of the Vietnam War and the Vatican was still uncomfortable with what they perceived as our excessive military zeal. Accordingly, Laird dutifully agreed to stay for the duration of the audience with the parked motorcade in the Vatican courtyard. Notwithstanding all this careful planning and agreement from both sides, when we were in the anteroom before the audience, a Vatican official came up to me and reported with horror the fact that the poor Secretary of Defense was just wandering around the Cortile di San Damaso alone, and would I please go get him and apologize for the rudeness of abandoning him there. This I did and that was the end of this unusual *contretemps*. The only other slight disturbance was the last minute request—once we were all in the anteroom—that the Secret Service wanted to make a security check of the pope's private bathroom. A few glares of disbelief from the Vatican officials and me quickly dispatched this exaggerated demand.

The visits of members of the cabinet required very limited planning on the protocol side but perhaps more on the substantive. In the five years I was in Rome, I handled a visit by Secretary of State William Rogers, two by Secretary Kissinger, and others by Treasury Secretaries Connally and Schultz. When I accompanied George Schultz on what was expected to be only a courtesy call, we were surprised that the Pope kept him for 30 minutes, during which time he questioned Schultz about the IMF meeting in Rome. The Pope expressed particular concern about the effects the energy crisis was likely to have on developing countries. We also managed to spirit Donald Rumsfeld and his wife into an audience while he was an aide at the White House.

With his impressive intellectual background and deep knowledge of history, Dr. Kissinger obviously relished his visits to the Vatican. He clearly appreciated that the Pope was highly informed and was a valid interlocutor on most current issues of world affairs. Pope Paul unquestionably had the longest experience in diplomacy of any world leader; he was always exceptionally well prepared, with a thick briefing book with colored tabs and talking points. Kissinger was at that time a true media star and was recognized everywhere he went in Rome and often cheered. As we were leaving the Vatican after his first visit, a group of Americans began to clap. Kissinger turned to Lodge and said in his droll, accented voice, "Maybe I should give them my blessing."

During Kissinger's second visit, on July 6, 1974, a rather elaborate control center was set up in the Hotel Excelsior on via Veneto, just across the street from the American Embassy. While making the customary arrangements with the Vatican, I was asked by Monsignor Monduzzi who would accompany Dr. Kissinger on his audience with the Pope and in particularly, whether Mrs. Kissinger would be present. I agreed to let Monduzzi know as soon as I had definite word, and we left it at that. Rather unexplainably, he then asked if Kissinger were a Catholic. I said, no, that he had been born into a German-Jewish family and that his wife was, I thought, an Episcopalian.

On the afternoon before the audience, I informed the Vatican that we still could not state precisely who would accompany Dr. Kissinger other than Lodge and myself. Once again they expressed the need to know about Nancy Kissinger as the protocol would be slightly different if she went along and once again, I could not get definite word.

At about 7 p.m., the control center informed me that I had an urgent telephone call from the Vatican. I picked up the phone and Monsignor Giovanni Re said that Archbishop Benelli had something very urgent to tell me. Benelli then came onto the line and said that he had a matter of the utmost delicacy to place in my hands: under no circumstances could the Pope receive Mrs. Kissinger. In the eyes of the Church the Kissingers were not married! Flabbergasted—not to say a bit terrified—I told him he couldn't be serious. Kissinger was not a Christian and his wife was not a Catholic. Benelli said he realized all that but as Jewish marriages were valid in the eyes of the Church, the Pope could not receive them together. I said that I expected that the problem would not arise, as Mrs. Kissinger had given no indication at this late date that she intended to go. However, if she did want to go I would have to tell the Secretary about the Vatican's position. Benelli agreed that if the worst came to pass, the Vatican's objections would have to be raised. After hanging up I decided that rather than biting the bullet myself and risk losing my head, the only prudent thing for me to do was to place this whole nettlesome matter into the hands of Lodge. Lodge jokingly told Kissinger that the Vatican didn't consider him and Nancy married. Kissinger laughed and said that it was no concern as Nancy was planning to go shopping anyway. Whether that was a face-saving remark, I cannot say for certain. We learned from our Vatican sources that, while in general, the Pope was very pleased with his meeting with Kissinger, he seemed a bit disappointed that Kissinger appeared unwilling to be drawn more fully into the question of Jerusalem.

The November 1973 visit of ex-Vice President Senator Hubert Humphrey was a lot of fun. He was free with his conversation and informed us fully on what was taking place in Washington. I went to quite a few sights and restaurants with him in Rome, and wherever we went, the Italians seemed to recognize him and greet him warmly. He was the most political animal one could find: campaigning non-stop even among the Romans. In restaurants he would walk into the kitchen and shake hands with and talk to all the cooks; he was truly a warm and engaging man.

Secretary of the Treasury John Connelly came to Rome in 1973 during the height of the financial crisis to discuss the future of exchange regulations and other pressing economic matters. He had no plans or desire to call on the Pope. He reportedly felt that this would be a waste of his precious time. Yet when the White House insisted that he call on the Pope, he complied. I accompanied a recalcitrant Connelly and his charming wife to the Vatican. He came out of his audience with a completely changed attitude, expressing his amazement over the degree of knowledge the Pope had of current events and admitted that the audience had been worthwhile indeed.

A man who frequently struck terror into the hearts of our embassies was Congressman John Rooney, Chairman of the House

Committee that dealt with the Department of State's budget. Rooney visited Rome in August 1971, and as a good Catholic, asked me to arrange a papal audience for him. I was aware that on previous visits Rooney had complained about some of the arrangements. Forewarned is forearmed, so I made a successful special effort to avoid repeating these problems. First, I briefed one of the Pope's aides on Rooney's assistance in getting almost $1 million to help repair Allied bomb-inflicted damage on the Papal Villas in Castel Gandolfo, and second, I found a good restaurant where the Chairman would not have to go up any steps. Rooney was delighted and left Rome better disposed to American diplomats than was often the case.

Visits from members of Congress can run anywhere from lots of fun to horror shows for American embassies. My experiences were generally positive, as I took the opportunity to gather useful information about what was going on in Washington. In some cases, the amount of money spent by Congressional delegations could border on the excessive. Some Congressmen were even known to engage in morally questionable entertainments while visiting foreign countries. There were always stories that some embassies kept carefully locked away files documenting the questionable antics of some Congressmen. Unfortunately, I never did find out whether these stories were accurate or just how these alleged files were to be used.

Pope Paul and Henry Kissinger,
with Robert Illing and Henry Cabot Lodge in the background

XI

Diplomatic Relations—Do We or Don't We?

Although rarely articulated outright, there was long a sharp difference of opinion between the Holy See and the United States as to whether or not diplomatic relations existed between the two. Everyone agreed that the United States had established only consular relations in 1797 and then moved to full diplomatic relations in 1848 when Jacob Martin presented his letters of accreditation as *chargé d'affaires* to Pope Pius IX. This arrangement continued with a number of ministers-resident until 1868 when the Congress declined to appropriate further funding for a mission to the Papal States. The argument at that time was that the Papal States were doomed to disappear and there was no point in wasting funds on a mission. The Papal States did, of course, cease to exist in 1870 with the conquest of Rome by the forces of the Kingdom of Italy.

The United States did not decide to send any further representatives to the Holy See until World War II when it was determined expedient that contacts with the pope could be useful in the war effort. Myron Taylor was President Roosevelt's choice as special representative to the Vatican, but at no time did the question arise of his being diplomatically accredited. The considered opinion in Washington was that despite the war, it was either imprudent or impossible to seek Senate confirmation for a representative to the Vatican due to residual but still significant anti-Catholic sentiment. A problem arose, however, once Italy had declared war on the United States. Taylor's assistant, Harold Tittmann, could not continue his residence in Rome where he had been working out of the U.S. Embassy. Like other countries at war with Italy, America desired to accept the hospitality of the Holy See and move Tittmann, his family, and secretary into the Vatican City. The Italians insisted though that U.S. could do so only if Tittmann were accorded full and proper diplomatic accreditation. This solution was finally agreed to by the United States and Tittmann was accredited formally as *chargé d'affaires.*

The position of Vatican lawyers on the question of United States relations with the Vatican was that relations had not been broken in 1868, but only placed in abeyance, figuratively put on ice. As stated earlier, a clear public indication of the Vatican's position was that in the *Annuario Pontificio* (the Vatican yearbook) the United States was always listed among the countries having diplomatic relations with the Holy See. Naturally, the names of American diplomatic representatives were left blank as no new representatives had been named.

The American contention that diplomatic relations were only established in 1984, when Ambassador William Wilson was named to the Vatican, is patently incorrect since relations had in reality never been broken by any overt act on the part of either side. In the final analysis, this was a case in which the United States, as has often been the case due to our "exceptionalism", refused to recognize the normal rules of established diplomatic practice under international law and in which both sides quietly agreed to disagree. Still, throughout this long period of over one hundred years, no damage was really done to the relationship and all agree that, Wilson was, of course, the first American Ambassador to the Holy See since all his 19th century predecessors had all been Ministers.

An amusing sidelight of this diplomatic duet was the fact that after 1870, the United States took no immediate steps to see to the closing of the various papal consulates in the U.S. A significant percentage of the first year's exchanges of diplomatic correspondence between Italy and the U.S. consisted of pleas from the Italians to move rapidly toward withdrawing the *exequaters* (the letter accrediting a consul)) of the papal consuls. The Italians argued quite logically that consulates could not exist from a state that had ceased to exist. As if viewing the matter from another planet, the U.S. State Department consistently failed to see the seriousness of the matter and occasionally noted that the consular incumbents representing the defunct Papal States were very nice men. American exceptionalism again seemed to raise its bizarre head.

The Lodge Mission makes a formal call on the Pope

XII

Our Diplomatic Relationship Under the Lodge Mission

The Pope and Vatican leadership were obviously delighted with the establishment of the Lodge Mission, which filled a long-vacant gap in the scope of Vatican access to world leaders. The Pope and his immediate staff loved to discuss world affairs and they jumped enthusiastically into exploiting their newly acquired linkage with America. It is interesting to consider just how the Vatican leadership viewed the United States. While it was clear that the United States was accepted by most people in the Vatican as a force for good in the world, and was certainly not in the same league as the most despised communist countries, there was nevertheless some reserve about the nature of American society and American actions in many foreign countries. While the Vatican certainly did not consider the United States a malignant force, it did doubt some American claims of religiousness or of being great practitioners of Judeo-Christian values. Just what do I mean by this seemingly unfair slur on our image?

Essentially, there are some basic distinctions between how the Catholic Church and how many Americans and the United States government view the Christian message. For Americans, Christianity would seem to focus mainly on personal beliefs and on private morality. For the Vatican, these aspects of Christianity are of central importance, but there is also a vast corpus of social values and policies, the social doctrines of the Church, running from the just distribution of wealth to a strong social safety net, that are also important. While these social doctrines are of great importance to the Church, Americans would generally label them as suspiciously socialistic. These social doctrines have roots going back to the late 19th century and were officially incorporated into Church thinking during the pontificate of Pope Leo XIII. By denigrating Catholic social policy as socialist, the United States has, in the eyes of the Church, eschewed what is accepted elsewhere as essential social policy. To put it bluntly, there is considerable mystification among Vatican officials, not to mention Europeans in general, as to how the United States missed the boat on what they consider basic ingredients of a modern, Western political commonwealth. I can assure my readers that this mystery is not easy to explain. I had been surprised to hear from several Vatican officials that they were not terribly concerned with poor church attendance in Europe since most European countries had managed to internalize the Christian message to such a degree that it was automatically reflected in their social policies. Thus, surprisingly to many Americans, a country of notoriously lax churchgoers like Sweden could be considered a very Christian country while the United States would be considered less so!

In spite of the above "mystification," the Vatican no doubt felt that they could work constructively with the United States on many issues of interest to them, obtain from us valuable and useful information on a wide range of subjects, and in general find common ground on a great number of problems afflicting the world. Notwithstanding, even though they might agree with us on our objectives, they were often critical of our methods. This, of course, was particularly true in Vietnam. *Faute-de-mieux*, they had little alternative but to deal with us. Yet I can easily believe that a very French-oriented man like Pope Paul VI may occasionally have wished that France and not the United States was the greatest superpower in the world.

Casaroli once told me that the Pope had remarked to him, "the diplomatic corps accredited here is like a marvelous piano on which we can play. You, Cardinal Villot. and Monsignor Benelli have a wonderful opportunity to play this instrument and hear the views of statesmen from around the world." Casaroli said that he advised the Pope to "play the piano more often."

The Vatican had impressive contacts throughout the world and they quickly proved willing to share with us information they obtained through these contacts, including some that were of quite a secretive nature. The Vatican provided very useful data from the Church leadership in North Vietnam, the Eastern European communist countries, and at times in China proper, although the PRC had show no disposition to reciprocate the Vatican's willingness for an open dialogue. Our talks and cooperation on development issues, especially in Latin America, were very valuable. Through AID (U.S. Aid for International Development), the U.S. Government was working to set up various cooperative ventures in Latin America together with the local Catholic leadership. One was a fisherman's cooperative in Peru, which Lodge was very interested in because of his personal relationship with Archbishop Marcos McGrath of Panama; another was a leadership-training center in Guatemala. The Nuncio in Guatemala helped in securing the release of a kidnapped American diplomat, and the Archbishop of Santo Domingo helped in the case of our kidnapped Air *attaché.*

On the eve of President Nixon's 1972 trip to Moscow, the Pope told Lodge that, "it was an event of worldwide significance and could be decisive for the life of nations." He noted that if the great powers can agree, then humanity's problems can be solved. His suggestion was that the great powers not forget the small countries, in particular the developing nations, and that, "they make up their minds to follow a policy of service and not a policy of power." Pope Paul was exceedingly impressed with the results of the President's Moscow visit.

The Italian media were notoriously adept at creative journalism, and Lodge's activities were frequently reported in a tendentious, highly imaginative, or out-rightly mendacious manner. A major offender was the weekly magazine *Panorama*. Highly popular with the Italian public, perhaps because of its amusingly inaccurate coverage, *Panorama* simply made up stories out of whole cloth. A friend of mine, who used to work for *Panorama* but left in disgust, told me that the magazine received reams of protest letters every month, many from people claiming not to have been anywhere near a given place at the time they were reported to have been there. He said that the magazine's publishers, Mondadori, were reportedly unhappy with the strong leftist element in *Panorama's* management. One might ask why this reported unhappiness did not lead to some change. The answer is possibly that the magazine earned such handsome revenues.

The Vatican had two newspapers: the semi-official daily *Osservatore Romano* and the unofficial weekly *Osservatore della Domenica.* The first was a paper of record to some degree, but as the Vatican identified it as *semi*-official, they could, if necessary fob off any article that might unexpectedly generate negative comment. The same principle applied to Vatican Radio and to the Vatican Press Office. When the latter's director Federico Alessandrini spoke officially it was official, but he often spoke on his own authority, thus releasing the Vatican from liability.

There were obviously occasional leaks of information, some of which were nettlesome. Those responsible for leaks appeared to be pushing their own particular agendas. There rarely seemed to be indiscriminate revelations even from the Pope's library (his office). As we discussed ever more delicate matters at the Vatican, the reliability of their security became more important to us. One possible weak point in their security might have been the domestic servants who waited on table at the Pope's frequent working lunches. Unlike most of his predecessors, Pope Paul was in the habit of eating with his close associates. We were not sure whether his household staff members were all clerics, but if there were laymen among them, the element of monetary motivation for passing information to the press became a possibility. A newspaper story that gave us much distress was one reporting that the Pope was outraged about the extent of American bombings in North Vietnam and that he had expressed his displeasure to the United States. The Vatican told us how enraged they were with this story and we expressed equal unhappiness, but in reality it was simply one of those situations in which each side knew where the truth lay but refrained from making a further issue of the matter.

A particularly interesting article about Karl Marx appeared in June 1972 in the *Osservatore della Domenica*. It was full of praise for Marx's exemplary virtues as a father and family man. His deep concern for the marriage prospects of his daughter Laura were given great prominence, notably his angered interventions with his future son-in-law about just what his financial capacity was, as Marx told him he was most anxious to avoid having his daughter suffer the poverty that his life's work had imposed on his beloved wife, Baroness Jenny von Westphalen. The objective of this article was to demonstrate that contemporary followers of Marx had seriously warped his beliefs concerning family life and child-rearing. The author pointed out that nothing could have been further from Marx's mind than the ideas on free love often associated with Marxism. It was certainly far from the writer's intent to give any sympathy to Marxist ideas in general.

There was no secret that Pope Paul and the Vatican leadership were strongly opposed to priests engaging in active or partisan politics, notably in holding public office. Jesuit Father Robert Drinan's election to the House of Representatives in 1970 was particularly galling to the Vatican. Shortly before the 1972 election, I was told that Cardinal Villot had asked the head of the Jesuit Order, Father Pedro Arrupe, to instruct his lost sheep Drinan not to run for re-election. Arrupe, who generally felt obliged to bend over backwards to prove he was "modern," was reluctant to comply in spite of the famous Jesuit centralized discipline and obedience to the Pope. After much anguished pondering in the Jesuit Curia, a telegram was finally sent to the superior of the Jesuit province of Massachusetts. It must not have been too convincing as Father Drinan continued his political career.

Lodge was firmly convinced that his arrangement of being resident in Rome only intermittently was best for the United States. He made a total of 14 visits during the five years I served as his assistant. He did not see any advantage in establishing diplomatic relations and told this to President Nixon and Secretary Kissinger.

The Lodge Mission was obtaining all the information possible from the Vatican and was achieving everything that full diplomatic missions could possibly achieve. Nothing would be gained from opening an embassy; it would cost much more and probably not provide enough concrete work to occupy an ambassador full time. Another advantage with the present arrangement was that the special envoy was frequently in Washington where he picked up the latest thinking on a wide variety of subjects of interest to the Vatican. Of course, Lodge was that truly rare and exceptional political appointee who had unusual access in Washington from the President on down and who had all the attributes of a professional diplomat. He was in every sense of the word a professional with unparalleled experience. The Pope showed himself willing to irritate many ambassadors accredited to the Holy See by seeing Lodge on each of his visits to Rome. Typically, an ambassador resident in Rome could only expect to see the Pope once a year. The Vatican admitted to us that they did receive complaints from some ambassadors about Lodge's access, but after all America was America. Some small embassies even expressed the fear to our Vatican contacts that their governments might even be tempted to close their embassies to the Holy See and set up something like the Lodge Mission.

XIII

Covering the Waterfront

The core function of any American diplomatic mission is reporting back to Washington. In the case of a small quasi-diplomatic outpost like the Lodge Mission, that essentially meant political reporting. Previously, Embassy Rome had designated an officer in its political section to cover the Vatican on a rather sporadic basis. When I arrived, I began to report on any activities that directly involved the Pope or the Vatican such as official high level visits to call on the Pope. Personally, I wanted to infuse my new job with as much substance as possible, so I soon began reporting on any activities of local Catholic churches worldwide that had political implications.

It was readily apparent to me that the Catholic Church had a useful, vast unofficial network for gathering information in any country where it was working, which basically included the entire world. I was able to quickly develop comfortable and useful give-and-take relationships with a vast number of officials of the Curia and other Vatican-related entities. After a short time, our office's reporting began to cover everything from the Vatican's efforts to reorient the Spanish Church in a more liberal direction to its efforts to place bishops of the Pope's choice in vacant sees in the European communist countries.

The political reporting from our little mission soon became voluminous. In most diplomatic missions, the bulk of political reporting deals with what is going on in the host country. Our situation was obviously quite different. The Vatican has long been considered—and rightly so—as a vast listening post, given its extensive contacts throughout most of the world, both through their diplomatic establishment as well as the even larger network of priests, who from time to time might provide local information of use to Rome. Thus, our mission immediately found itself reporting on literally scores of countries throughout the entire world, drawing on information provided to us by a wide range of contacts within the Vatican. Our most important contacts were the members of the Council of Public Affairs of the Secretariat of State, an entity virtually analogous to the foreign ministry of a secular government. Most members of staff were career diplomats, often with considerable on-the-ground experience in the countries they dealt with. The Vatican diplomatic establishment was lopsidedly Italian, but with an increasing number of other nationalities repre-sented, including a number of Americans. All of the staff placed a high value on discretion. Once my interlocutors were reassured as to our office's reliability to be discreet, many new doors began to open. In the noteworthy case of securing Cardinal Mindszenty's departure from Hungary, which took over six months of careful four-way negotiations among the Hungarian Government, Mindszenty, the Vatican, and the United States Government, our discretion gained us singular admiration.

ASIA

Vietnam

Of the dozens of countries we covered in our reporting, none was more important during my five years in Rome than Vietnam. Given the relatively large Catholic population in Vietnam, which went back to the first French efforts at evangelization almost four hundred years ago, the Vatican had profound involvement in the country. The North Vietnamese had utilized typical communist tactics to weaken and divide the local Catholic Church, such as the creation of a "patriotic church" and the placing of obstacles in the way of communication between the Vatican and local bishops. Given these circumstances, the Vatican would clearly have preferred a victory by the South Vietnamese, whose leadership included practicing Catholics and was generally sympathetic to the Church and its activities in their country. In this regard, the United States and the Vatican were on the same side. In fact, the Vatican generally approved of our stated objectives in Vietnam, but frequently questioned our methods, which they found excessively aggressive and hence often counterproductive. While the Vatican hoped that America might succeed in guaranteeing the survival of the South, they often doubted that this was realistic.

One might have assumed that the Vatican, dedicated openly to the preservation of human life, might have opposed the type of brutal warfare taking place in Vietnam, regardless of its alleged justification. That did not, however, appear to be the case. To a certain extent, it appeared that the Vatican associated communism with the numerous heresies that had plagued the Church throughout its long history and viewed America's crusade against international communism as analogous to the witch-hunts of the Inquisition. Something like killing the heretical believer to save his soul! One British expert on the Vatican, Peter Nichols, has written that the Vatican was outraged that President Nixon had sent Cabot Lodge, a man so intimately associated with the horrors of Vietnam, as his envoy. Frankly, I never got the slightest inkling that any of our contacts harbored such feelings—quite the contrary.

At every possible opportunity and at every conceivable level, starting with Cabot Lodge's first visit in July 1970, we discussed Vietnam and related issues with the Vatican. The United States had actually been in contact with the Vatican on Vietnam since the early years of the war, when, in fact, Lodge, as Ambassador in Saigon, called on Pope Paul in May 1965. While in Saigon, Lodge had frequent conversations with the Papal Nuncio and later, while heading the Paris Peace Talks, Lodge frequently communicated with the Papal Nuncio to France, who tried to be helpful in moving the talks in a positive direction. Before the Lodge Mission, these high level meetings tended to be intermittent. With our mission, they became institutionalized, regular and frequent exchanges of information and outlooks.

From the outset, our major efforts connected with the Vietnam War could be divided into the following categories:

Improving the flow of communications with our prisoners-of-war held by the North Vietnamese;

Frequently briefing the Vatican on the situation in Vietnam from our viewpoint;

Obtaining information from the Vatican on their relations with Vietnam, especially their contacts with the North;

Trying to forestall any public statements by the Vatican harmful to U.S. policy.

The Vatican was generally sympathetic with the United States' professed goals in Vietnam but from time to time did not find out methods highly praiseworthy. The Vatican found the United States to be excessively zealous in the bombing of certain strategic targets. On two occasions, the Pope called me in late at night to issue a protest over the bombings. Even the Soviet statesman Gromyko had expressed to the Pope his belief that both China and the Democratic Republic of Vietnam were deeply worried about the United States' long-range intentions in Asia.

Pope Paul VI and a number of Vatican officials had been actively engaged in the Vietnam peace process going back at least to 1965. In December of that year, the Pope helped in bringing about the 1965 Christmas truce in Vietnam. In 1966, the Pope repeatedly expressed his willingness to be of assistance in arranging peace talks. Apostolic Delegate in Tehran Monsignor Salvatore Asta successfully requested the Shah to intervene with the governments of Pakistan, Romania, and Yugoslavia in an effort to seek a solution in Vietnam.

During this period, the Vatican made fruitless efforts to make contact with Hanoi. When he met with Soviet President Podgorny in January 1967, Pope Paul asked him to advise the North Vietnamese to halt their military infiltrations into South Vietnam. He also asked Podgorny to use the USSR's good offices on behalf of opening negotiations. On February 8, the Pope sent a telegram to Ho Chi Minh asking that he call a truce for the Tet holidays. In December 1967, following the Pope's offer to send a mission to North Vietnam to visit prisoner-of-war camps, we were told that the Vatican had been unable to obtain entry permits to the DRV in the past and probably could not obtain them now. In January 1968, the Vatican informed us that President Nyerere of Tanzania had written the Pope about contacts that he had had with North Vietnam and claiming that the North was prepared to negotiate with the United States if the bombing halted. On April 30, the Vatican formally informed the United States Embassy at Rome that they were offering to provide a site for any eventual peace talks. A few days later, President Johnson wrote the Pope expressing his thanks for the offer to house peace talks, but informing the Pope that a Paris site had been decided upon.

The Vatican made continuous efforts on behalf of our POWs, but finally in early 1968, the North Vietnamese replied that our prisoners of war were war criminals and therefore the Geneva Accords did not apply to them. Archbishop Casaroli made a number of visits to Paris where he spoke to Mai Van Bo, North Vietnam's representative in Paris, and to Madame Binh about our prisoners of war. This relationship was also continued by the Papal Nunciature in Paris on a several occasions. The Vatican told us in 1970 that they would be willing to set up a special mission in the DRV to deal with our prisoners if the North would permit this.

Over the years, Pope Paul made a great number of public appeals for peace in Vietnam. His statements were detached, sincere, and by and large, balanced. These peace initiatives on behalf of Vietnam did much to establish his credentials as one of the world's leading neutral peacemakers. The Vatican firmly believed that Hanoi's conviction that the Pope was a genuinely neutral peacemaker induced Xuan Thuy to make his call on the Pope in February 1973.

We assiduously followed Vatican contacts with the North Vietnamese and their many efforts to improve the status of the Catholic Church in areas controlled by the North. This included numerous efforts to offer aid to North Vietnam, especially through various Catholic charitable organizations like Caritas.

The continuing hostility of the Northern leaders to the Vatican led to a great deal of gloom in Rome, and by mid-1972 it became clear that the Vatican had pretty much given up any hope in an American victory. This was most notably reflected in the fact that virtually no funding was allocated to missionary activities in the South. A written-off church for the moment!

The Lodge Mission took considerable pride in the fact that, out of all our diplomatic establishments dealing with friendly powers, we seemed to be one of the few that managed to keep the host country's outspokenness on events in Vietnam within acceptable limits. Especially during the numerous heavy bombings, the Vatican felt tempted, and in fact was pressured by others, to speak out more sharply than they did. We believed that our frequent talks with Benelli and Casaroli went a long way in restraining them.

The tensest moments in my entire five years in Rome came when the United States resumed heavy bombing north of the 20th parallel. The most anguished event was on Christmas Eve 1973, when the United States bombed Hai Phong Harbor. I had just attended a midnight mass in the Sistine Chapel, when Casaroli approached me with a long face. He asked that I call immediately at his apartment in the Vatican Gardens as he had an important message for President Nixon from the Pope. I dutifully drove over to his house in the pouring rain and was ushered in to his sitting room. He proceeded to inform me that the Pope was outraged and deeply saddened that we had chosen to resume heavy bombing on Christmas Eve. The Pope had asked him to call me in to protest this ill-advised act and also to call in Soviet Ambassador Ryzhov to ask that his government take any steps it could to minimize the damage and limit the response from both the DRV and China. Suitably humbled, I raced over to the Embassy to send a back-channel telegram to the White House for the President that contained the Pope's sharp protest. While I remained completely circumspect at the time, I did think that the choice of Christmas Eve was totally ham-handed. My only request to Casaroli was that no public mention be made of the Pope's protest. In this regard, the Vatican maintained total silence.

I repeatedly pointed out to our contacts how regrettable it was that many of our European friends found it so easy to believe North Vietnamese propaganda and to forget what the North Vietnamese and their allies were doing in South Vietnam, not to mention in Cambodia and Laos. Casaroli admitted that Hanoi had been terribly successful in winning the propaganda battle. Unfortunately, he said, in such a conflict as the Vietnam War where the world's greatest power is pitted against a small underdeveloped country, human nature tends naturally to side with the underdog. Late one night, I discussed with Casaroli Hanoi's claim that 1300 persons had been killed during our latest bombing. I pointed out that had our bombing been as extensive as Hanoi claimed and directed primarily against populated areas, this number could easily have been five times as great. Casaroli admitted that Hanoi's claims of the concentrated bombing on populated areas seemed ridiculous.

In January 1973, Luigi Bettazzi, the Bishop of Ivrea near Turin, announced that he would be travelling to Hanoi with a "Study Group" of the Stockholm Conference on Vietnam. The announcement reportedly made quite a stir in the Turin area, which was notably left wing and generally critical of U.S. policies in Vietnam. Following a timely call I made on Monsignor Luigi Dossena, the Vietnam Desk Officer in the Secretariat of State, I was informed categorically that the bishop would not be travelling to Hanoi. The next day, Bettazzi announced that prior commitments made it impossible for him to visit Vietnam.

Following South Vietnamese President Thieu's audience with the Pope, I asked "Deputy Foreign Minister" Monsignor Mario Pio Gaspari whether the Pope would mention this meeting at his mass general audience later the same morning. I stressed that it would not be balanced to avoid mentioning his meeting with Thieu when the Pope had announced with great joy his meeting with Xuan Thuy of North Vietnam. Gaspari telephoned back in a half-hour to say that the Pope intended only to address the tenth anniversary of Pope John's encyclical *Pacem in Terris*. After the audience I checked with the Vatican press office and was told that the Pope had departed from the prepared text and made a surprise reference to meeting with Thieu, not mentioning him by name but leaving no doubt to whom he referred. It was impossible to determine whether our timely intervention prompted the Pope's reference to Thieu, but I felt it was quite likely.

The Vatican was keenly aware of the deteriorating military situation in South Vietnam, especially based on detailed reporting from their Papal Nuncio in Saigon, Archbishop Henri Lemaitre. On August 29, 1974, Casaroli had me called in to discuss a particularly gloomy report they had just received from Lemaitre, and asked whether the United States could provide the Pope with an up-to-date assessment of the current situation. Lemaitre had reported that bishops in the northern border regions of South Vietnam were terrified that the military balance had tilted seriously in favor of the Viet Cong. The bishops estimated that at least 100,000 new refugees had fled, expanding the area under Viet Cong control, and that the pace of kidnapping, notably of young people and of village leaders, had greatly increased. Moreover, the bishops suspected a vastly increased presence of DRV troops. Needless to say, during his next visit, Lodge provided the Pope with the desired assessment.

It was not only the Vatican that had given up hope on an American victory in Vietnam. The Taiwanese Ambassador, Chen Chihmai, informed me that his Vatican and European contacts had all expressed deep concern over America's ability to effectively exercise its power. He considered it a great error that we did not cut our losses in Vietnam and leave earlier. He quoted an old Chinese proverb, which says: truly wise is the man who cuts off his arm to save his life. He noted that his own country fought a foolish, hopeless, and unnecessary war with Japan over Manchuria and that it would have been far better to have let Manchuria go. Archbishop Casaroli mentioned to me that the Pope found it tragic that the United States was losing its traditionally good reputation in its fights to defend worthy causes, while the forces of tyranny and oppression seem to be getting better press.

On May 8, 1972, I delivered a message to the Pope from President Nixon announcing our intention to mine the entrances to all North Vietnamese ports and to interdict all rail and other transportation. The Pope was informed that these actions would stop when an internationally-supervised cease-fire began throughout Vietnam and all prisoners of war were released. The President further promised to cease all United States military activity in Vietnam and to withdraw all U.S. forces from Vietnam within four months. These actions were not taken to impose a defeat but rather to end the conflict and to permit a settlement through negotiations. Following the mining, Archbishop Casaroli called me at home where I was nursing a serious flu complete with high temperatures. He asked me to come to his apartment in the Vatican Gardens to receive an urgent message from the Pope. The Pope was, he said, profoundly preoccupied over what was happening in Vietnam. The Pope accepted that our reasons for being in Vietnam, that is to say fighting for the right of a small nation to exist freely and independently, were entirely idealistic, moral, and justified. However, the Pope's concern was the risk of a great power confrontation involving the Soviet Union. The Pope was willing to take whatever steps were useful, either public or private, including making a public declaration. He made this offer out of an interest for peace and out of friendship for the United States. Casaroli noted moreover that he would be discussing this issue with Soviet Ambassador Ryzhov. Casaroli was his characteristically cool self and gave me the clear impression that the Pope understood our reasons for mining the harbors, but that he was nonetheless worried about the possibility of a great power confrontation.

I believe that since Soviet Foreign Trade Minister Patolichev had called on President Nixon *following* our mining announcement there was little concern about possible Soviet overreaction. And indeed, Casaroli subsequently told me that, after speaking to me, he had discussed the question with Ambassador Ryzhov, who had reassured him that the Soviets had no intention of taking any strong steps against the American decision to mine the harbors. Casaroli had attempted to reassure the Pope, but the Pope insisted he call Ryzhov and me in on the same night.

A number of my Vatican contacts, including newspapermen, noted that in the late 1960s, there was considerable suspicion over the United States' positions on Vietnam, but that in the last few years, that opposition to our stated objectives had mellowed considerably. These changes were probably due to two factors. The first was the realization that the North Vietnamese were not possessed of much good will in their negotiating posture *vis-à-vis* the United States and the second was that our Lodge Mission had been able to provide the Vatican with a constant and well-presented stream of material on our positions.

As many top Vatican officials appeared to work around the clock, I occasionally got called for a conversation at unusual hours. One such incident was on the night of December 30, 1972, when Casaroli asked me to come to his office. He expressed the Pope's satisfaction with the President's announcement that he would suspend the bombing North of the 20th parallel, and that the peace negotiations would be resumed in Paris on January 2. Casaroli pointed out that the Pope would no doubt wish to publicly express his pleasure over the bombing halt. He said he did not suspect that the United States would mind if the Pope made passing reference to having previously expressed his wishes for a bombing halt to the United States Government. I noted that there was considerable value in maintaining the secrecy of the present channel, but noted that should the Pope feel it desirable to mention having expressed his views to us, he should likewise note that he did the same to the DRV. Casaroli expressed his agreement, but said he would appreciate knowing how strongly the United States Government felt on this matter. I promised to seek an official reaction, but noted that the Vatican's earlier denial of a Papal message to the President had been borne out. Casaroli admitted that he had to agree. After checking with the Department of State, I informed Casaroli that the bombing halt had gone into effect on December 30 and that we had no objection to the Pope noting his interventions with the parties on this matter, provided that he made clear that he had done so with both sides.

During a conversation on February 5, 1975, Casaroli took the initiative to express the Vatican's anguished concern over the prospects for the survival of democracy in South Vietnam. He asked if United States Government thought that South Vietnam could maintain itself against its communist adversaries. He mentioned that in recent conversation, the Republic of Vietnam Ambassador, Nguyen Van Hieu, had told him that without the requested $300 million of additional U.S. aid, it was very doubtful that the RVN could manage to hold out for the remainder of the year. Casaroli then recalled that during Secretary Kissinger's November 5, 1974 discussions with Pope Paul, the Pope had expressed his hope that the United States would not abandon South Vietnam. Secretary Kissinger, Casaroli also recalled, had assured Pope Paul that the U.S. administration was committed to continuing assistance for Vietnam, but that Congressional concurrence was necessary and increasingly difficult to obtain. I assured Casaroli that the Administration remained firmly committed to assisting Vietnam and fervently hoped that Congress would agree to the latest aide request. While I could not assess RVN's chances for continuing resistance without our additional aid, I stressed that in the two years since the Paris Accords, and despite the increasing number of violations from the North, the South Vietnamese had made impressive gains in strengthening their defenses and bolstering their economy. Casaroli agreed but feared that the balance may be irretrievably shifting against the democratic forces. Unfortunately, he added, an international press campaign against South Vietnam and President Thieu had caused great damage. The Church looked upon President Thieu as the legally and democratically consti-tuted government and for that reason felt justified in giving him its support. At the end of the conversation Casaroli confessed that the Vatican now had to give serious consideration to the possi-bility of changing its whole approach to Vietnam, especially if the cause really appeared to be lost. It would involve a massive change in the missionary policy as well.

After this jeremiad it was clear that we had to scamper to give the Pope the kind of concrete reassurances he was crying out for. Lodge dutifully—but probably not too convincingly—did this during his next visit.

By 1975, it was obvious to all but the most delusional in Washington that the war in Vietnam was irretrievably lost. The Vatican continued to ask the uncomfortable questions that reality compelled them to ask and we continued to provide them with the falsely optimistic assessments that we felt compelled to provide. We were all engaged in an elegant but empty charade. After each briefing, I left the Vatican with the hope that our arguments had been convincing but knowing in my heart what we all knew: there was no hope of victory.

The final anguished appeal from the Pope took place on March 28 when Benelli called Ambassador Lodge to his office for a 9:45 p.m. meeting to deliver a verbal message from the Pope on the condition of the refugees in Vietnam. The Pope warned that if something was not done within 24 hours, catastrophe was certain. There were 600,000 in Danang alone and their evacuation was an urgent necessity. "I plead to you, Mr. President, to make every effort to save these miserable people," the Pope ended. Lodge said that the U.S. fully shared the Pope's concern over the refugees, and that we were exploring every way of alleviating the suffering and transporting the refugees to safer areas. Lodge ended by assuring Benelli that he would deliver the papal message to the President.

Two months later, on May 8, President Ford answered the Pope's message, saying that he fully shared the Pope's concern over the refugees and assuring that every effort would be made to assist those displaced by the recent tragic events in Vietnam. The President informed the Pope that since receiving his message, the U.S. had evacuated nearly 60,000 refugees from threatened areas of Vietnam. He mentioned his appeals to other countries to help with settling refugees and sought the Pope's assistance in encouraging other countries to help with this massive humanitarian effort. The Pope communicated his gratitude to the President in a private message on June 1.

As the United States was evacuating Vietnam, a peculiar disagreement of a philosophical nature arose between the United States and the Vatican over our right to bring Vietnamese orphans to the United States. Benelli told me that he had given strict instructions to Caritas and other Catholic charitable agencies to keep their hands strictly off the Vietnam airlift of orphans. He said he was fully aware that the American Government and American families were accepting orphans from entirely praiseworthy motives; however, the Holy See opposed the whole movement on the principle that any child had the God-given right to be raised in the country of his ancestry. In response I said that such a concept was difficult for Americans to understand, and that seeing the bleak future that confronted these children and the willingness of Vietnamese officials to permit their departure, we felt morally and humanitarianly moved to do what we could for them. Moreover, I pointed out, the bulk of the orphans brought to America were of mixed parentage, many children being the illegitimate offspring of Americans serving in Vietnam. I noted that surely his principle did not apply to them. Once more he flabbergasted me by saying that, yes, it did, since their mothers were presumably still in Vietnam. We ended the conversation by agreeing that the American and Italian philosophical concepts of the problem were totally irreconcilable but that no ill will was meant on either side.

China

While China did not play a large role in our reporting from the Vatican, there were occasional flurries of interest. Prior to the Pope's Asia trip in the fall of 1970, the press began reporting an increase of Vatican interest in ties with Beijing. Several rumors that the Pope would visit Hong Kong were brought to my attention, and as one might have expected, they turned out to be unfounded. Likewise the transfer of Pro-Nuncio Luigi Accogli from Taipei to Ecuador was viewed in some quarters as a gesture toward the PRC when in reality it was simply a routine reposting.

During my entire five years in Rome, the Republic of China maintained an Ambassador at the Vatican, Chen Chihmai. After the U.N. voted to seat the PRC as the representative of China, Chen's position in Rome became a bit more difficult. He did, however, continue unofficial relations with other missions to the Vatican even after their governments had ceased to maintain diplomatic ties with Taiwan and shifted them to Beijing. Chen told me that a number of Western European countries had suggested that Taiwan not break diplomatic relations with them but merely "suspend" them, so that a semblance of official communications could be maintained. In the case of the Vatican, Chen had been assured by its top officials that no change in its relationship with the ROC was contemplated.

Although he had naturally been out of mainland China for a long time, he was nevertheless very well informed about the PRC and its top personalities. When we came to discuss President Nixon's trip to China, his overriding preoccupation was that the President might make some arrangements or agreements with persons whose futures in China were not secure. He feared that Nixon would return home believing he had begun long-term bilateral relations only to find the whole edifice collapse at the fall of, for example, Chou Enlai. Ambassador Chen considered Chou the most reasonable and attractive man in the PRC, but feared that as merely the leader of the bureaucracy, his power base was considerably limited when compared with that of other potential leaders who enjoyed party and military support. Chen compared Chou's reputation with that of Madame Chiang Kaishek, both of whom were considerably more important and well-known abroad than in their respective countries. Given Chou's age and lack of wide backing, Chen felt genuine concern about the lasting value of any agreements he might make with the U.S.

When the United Nations again took up the question of Chinese representation, a number of countries, including ourselves, attempted to obtain Vatican support for our position on seeking no changes that would unseat Taiwan. The hope was that the Vatican would use its influence with a number of countries to support the U.S. resolution. The Vatican would probably have welcomed the entry of the PRC at the expense of their "old friends" in Taiwan. This would have untied their hands in the eventuality of representation when and if the time ever came for them to open some sort of mission in Beijing. The Vatican had always privately expressed willingness—if not a desire—to open wide-ranging discussions with the PRC. They explained to us that only if the question of relations became a distinct possibility would they begin to examine how to handle future ties with the ROC on Taiwan. As a matter of fact, there was a great deal of speculation in late 1972 when Papal Pro-Nuncio Edward Cassidy was away from Taipei in his native home of Australia for ten months. The Vatican did in fact inform me that his lengthy absence was indeed a gesture to the PRC. They had decided to reassign Cassidy and henceforth leave the Taipei office in the hands of a *chargé d'affaires*, but had no intention of severing diplomatic relations with the ROC. Emphasis in the future, however, would be with the "Church in Taiwan" rather that with the government. The Church leaders on Taiwan had come to accept the necessity of the Vatican preparing itself for that probably distant day when better relations might become possible with the PRC. That, of course, did not come to pass during my five years in Rome.

In November 1971, Casaroli told me that Norman Cousins, former editor of the *Saturday Review*, had sought meetings in the Vatican as part of his plan to dedicate himself full-time to private efforts for the settlement of international differences. Cousins, who had established good relations with Khruschev, was instrumental in 1963 in obtaining the release from prison of the Ukrainian Cardinal Joseph Slipyj. Cousins now planned to visit Beijing and had reported to the Vatican that he had discussed his forthcoming trip with Secretary Kissinger. Casaroli then asked me if I could get a confirmation that Kissinger had indeed seen Cousins. I discussed with Ambassador Martin whether to send the Casaroli's request to the Department by cable or by letter. Ambassador Martin felt that since we would not wish to facilitate or encourage Vatican contacts with the PRC, it was best to send a letter and tell Casaroli that we had not yet heard should he inquire the following week. Thus cynicism won the day.

In December of 1970, the visit to Canton by two Italian missionary priests caused quite a stir in the Italian press. Casaroli denied to me that anyone in the top levels of the Vatican had prior knowledge of the visit, but he did not exclude that someone in the vast Vatican apparatus may have been aware of it. He admitted surprise, however, over the rapidity with which the People's Republic of China had issued the visas, noting that "in their Chinese minds they may have considered the two priests to be Vatican envoys." He carefully pointed out that any speculation that the Pope was attempting to serve as a channel for bringing China into the community of nations was highly fanciful. He observed that it would be foolish and preposterous for the Pope to attempt a role completely beyond his power and also quite obviously unacceptable to the Chinese. The Vatican may have been willing, under the right circumstances, to lend its good offices in bilateral disputes wherein both parties believed that the Vatican's neutral position could be helpful, but only on moral or humanitarian grounds. Casaroli closed his remarks with the established Vatican position that it was, of course, folly to keep a large and important country like China indefinitely out of major international bodies like the U.N.

When President Nixon's impending visit to the PRC was announced in July 1971, the Vatican made its first comment in an unsigned editorial in the semi-official daily newspaper *L'Osservatore Romano* on July 18, the tone of which was one of great satisfaction. The article expressed the hope that the meeting would be a "great contribution to collaboration between peoples and therefore to the cause of peace." At his noon public address at his summer residence at Castel Gandolfo, the Pope noted that international events called our attention. He asked, "What is happening and what will happen in the world? Something great and new completes itself and prepares itself, which can change considerably the face of the earth. We will also have something to say, some hope to express, but not now, not here." Our Vatican sources clarified that the Pope's rather cryptic declaration that he had more yet to say did not presage any startling announcements on Sino-Vatican relations. We were firmly assured that there was nothing on the horizon in regard to relations with the PRC. Their position was that for the time being there was no alternative to accepting the fiction of one Chinese nation with two states. In any case, even were relations of some nature possible, the Holy See would not wish to do anything that would prejudice their excellent ties with Taiwan, where the Church was flourishing nicely. Since the PRC seemed a long way from considering any meaningful relaxation of its strongly negative policy on believers, there were really no grounds for hope on any contacts at that time.

The Dalai Lama paid a low-key private visit to Rome for five days in late September 1973. During his visit, the Dalai Lama had a 30-minute private audience with Pope Paul, who limited himself in his public announcement to welcoming his visitor as a purely religious figure and eschewing any references to his political significance. Cardinal Sergio Pignedoli later told me that the visit was merely fraternal in nature. He even downplayed the Dalai Lama's influence within the Buddhist world, noting that the recent visits by leaders of Thai and Laotian Buddhist communities were more important in the context of worldwide Buddhism.

Philippines

A Pope would normally receive the chief-of-state of a Catholic country or their family members in a private audience, but when Imelda Marcos, the wife of the Philippine President Ferdinand Marcos, came to Rome in mid-February 1973, that was not considered politic. By that time, the Marcos regime had revealed its dictatorial flavor and the Vatican did not wish to make any gesture that gave the impression that they looked even with the most minimal favor on Marcos and company. The decision taken was merely to grant Mrs. Marcos a five-minute special audience in which she was sandwiched in among a series of other groups having similar brief special audiences. This could only have been understood by President Marcos as a blow to his prestige and a snub. When I discussed the matter later with Monsignor Gaspari, his tone revealed considerable apprehension in the Vatican concerning the course of Philippine politics. It was clear that granting Mrs. Marcos only a special audience was intended as an indication of papal disfavor for her husband's most recent political policies. The fact that the politically conscious Mrs. Marcos did not inform the local press of her audience and its length—an important factor with papal audiences—would have seemed to indicate that she herself may have gotten the message.

Pakistan

The first Vatican comment on the developing independence movement in East Pakistan came in an article by press spokesman

Federico Alessandrini in the unofficial weekly *L'Osservatore della Domenica* on April 4, 1971. The article singled out the "hard and indiscriminate character of repression" on the part of the Pakistan Government. Alessandrini pointed out that the central government's general neglect of development in the east had fueled the independence movement and led to the election victory of the Awami League in December 1970. While mentioning that is was very difficult to comment on the basis of the limited amount of information available, the article claimed, "but what is known leads one to wonder whether fundamental human rights are being respected."

On December 29, 1971, shortly before the ceasefire of the Indo-Pakistan War, Cardinal Jean Villot, the Secretary of State, sent a message in the Pope's name to the Pro-Nuncio in New Delhi, Monsignor John Gordon, asking him to intercede with the Indian Government and request that they seek to guarantee the safety of civilians in East Pakistan. He further requested that all Catholic institutions be respected and that they be permitted to accept refugees irrespective of religious affiliation.

Following a private audience of two bishops from Bangladesh with the Pope on February 20, 1972, the Vatican informed us that they had no immediate intention to recognize the newly independent country but would let the process toward recognition develop in a gradual and natural manner. The Vatican would begin by sending a special representative to Bangladesh to investigate the aftermath of the war and its effect on the Catholic community. My source said that normally the nuncio from a neighboring country would be chosen for such a mission, but that under the circumstances, it was impossible to send a nuncio from either New Delhi or Islamabad; therefore, it was most likely that someone would go directly from the Vatican. The representative was expected to carry a message addressed to the Bangladeshi President from either the Pope or the Cardinal Secretary of State. To avoid damaging its good relations with West Pakistan, the Vatican intended to discuss beforehand with the Pakistanis its intention to send the mission to Dacca, placing the emphasis on the purely religious nature of the visit. Any move toward formal diplomatic recognition of Bangladesh and the stationing of a nuncio in Dacca would have to await the stabilization of relations between Islamabad and Dacca.

In early 1973, Vatican assistance was sought on behalf of the Pakistani prisoners of war still remaining in Indian hands following the cessation of hostilities. The Pakistani Embassy to the Holy See informed me that they had made a *démarche* asking the Vatican to intercede with India to obtain better treatment for the prisoners, who had been held for over one year. However, the Vatican demurred as they considered the question too delicate at that time for them to become involved with it. The Pakistani effort continued on April 11 when the wives of four Pakistani prisoners of war had a special audience with Pope Paul. The audience received no publicity.

Shortly after this visit, the Indian Ambassador to the Holy See, Arjan Singh, came from his residence in Bern, Switzerland, to call on contacts at the Vatican. While in Rome, he asked that the Vatican consider a mediating role in the dispute in the subcontinent. At this time, he noted that it would be impossible for India to consider the return of the prisoners of war. Pakistan would first need to recognize Bangladesh. Various Vatican officials told Singh that it was distinctly unfair to make the prisoners pawns in such political bargaining, and that moreover the Vatican refused any mediating role on the grounds that the whole issue was too highly political for them to become involved in at that moment.

Cambodia

A highly distressed Deputy Secretary of State, Archbishop Giovanni Benelli, called me to his office on March 19, 1975, to inform me that the Pope was deeply anguished over the situation in Cambodia. The Apostolic Delegate in Saigon, Archbishop Henri Lemaitre, had sent in reports to the Vatican in the previous few days which indicated that the Khmer Rouge were wantonly massacring innocent civilians in the areas that they had recently conquered. These reports from Lemaitre were based on information obtained from Catholic clergy in combat areas as well as from other reliable sources. Benelli said that the Pope was anxiously hoping the U.S.

Government could make some effort to limit the bloodshed then under way in Cambodia. The Pope did not presume to suggest just what exactly the U.S. Government could do. In answer to Benelli, I said that President Ford and his Administration had for months been trying to alert public opinion to the likelihood of serious communist reprisals in Cambodia and for this reason we have sought additional assistance for the legitimate Lon Nol Government. Our Congress, however, did not appear in any way disposed to vote the requested funding. Benelli closed by reporting that in Pope Paul's name, Cardinal Secretary of State Villot had sent telegrams of concern to the Apostolic Vicar of Phnom Penh and to the Bishop of Ban Me Thuot in the neighboring Republic of Vietnam.

Korea

By mid-1974, the increasingly authoritarian environment in South Korea under President Park's control began to inspire attacks from a few Catholic leaders in the country, notably Bishop Daniel Chi of Wonju. It was clear to the Vatican that Chi had indeed given $3000 to a dissident Catholic poet, Kim Chi Hak. The government accused Chi of having given the money to a dissident organization that the poet belonged to and not just to the poet himself. The Vatican's initial impression was that Chi would not be formally charged but would be sent back to his diocese and perhaps held under house arrest for a period of time. Regrettably, this did not happen. A reliable Vatican source told me that he believed that Chi was purposefully engaging in provocative actions against the government in the hope that he would be arrested and become a "cause célèbre," thus attracting heavy media attention both in Korea and abroad. It was Chi's hope that such attention would bring pressure on the Korean government for reforms.

By late July when it became apparent that the GOK had every intention of charging Chi with illegal activities against the government, the Vatican became deeply anxious about Chi's eventual fate. Pro-Nuncio Luigi Dossena managed only to obtain the GOK's agreement to postpone Chi's trial for one week until

August 1. Both Dossena and the Vatican were convinced that Chi, who was well know for his "excessive zeal," was determined to make a martyr of himself in the hope of calling attention to the abridgement of civil liberties in South Korea, and, ideally, to make a substantial contribution to their improvement. It would have been convenient for the Vatican to have been able to call Chi back to Rome for consultations, but this was out of the question. Chi had just been to Rome, receiving advice from the Pope and everyone else against involvement in organized political affairs. The Vatican felt that any right-thinking person could easily support Bishop Chi's positions, but they feared that his activities could redound to the disadvantage of the Church in Korea.

On August 6, the Vatican Radio broadcast an appeal for Chi's liberation. Monsignor Achille Silvestrini informed me on August 8 that he had been in touch with the Korean Ambassador to the Holy See Shin, who had recently returned to Rome. The Ambassador allowed that he was aware of the inherent dangers for Government of the Republic of Korea relations with Catholics and Christians in general should the case of Bishop Chi get out of hand. He told the Vatican that while he was in Seoul he did everything possible to impress upon his government the degree of prestige which a bishop enjoys in the Catholic Church and the danger involved in bringing a bishop to trial.

In late August, following Chi's being sentenced to prison, the Vatican decided it best to remain quiescent for some time in order to let the dust settle in the general Korean political environment. The harshness of the sentence was a shock to the Vatican. Archbishop Casaroli called in Korean Ambassador Shin to inform him of the Pope's deep sorrow over the sentence. Casaroli asked that the Government of the Republic of Korea take into consideration Bishop Chi's delicate physical condition. My sources anticipated that within a few months the GORK might come up with an imaginative face-saving solution, which would permit the commutation of Chi's sentence. Notwithstanding, our sources were not convinced that the Vatican would agree if such a GORK proposal included Chi's transfer out of South Korea.

On October 12, Korean Foreign Minister Kim met with Secretary of State Cardinal Villot for a *tour d'horizon* of major bilateral matters. Regarding foreign missionaries, Villot made clear the Vatican's position that foreign missionaries are guests in the host country and therefore should conform to behavior incumbent on any non-citizen, which included refraining from involvement in domestic political affairs. Conversely, the Vatican has no intention of ordering or attempting to coerce the native Korean hierarchy to remain aloof from domestic affairs. As a principle, the Vatican frowns on local Church involvement in "political activities" such as partisan matters and electoral campaigning, but it leaves it up to the local churchmen to decide just what constitute "political activities." Villot avoided an appeal for Bishop Chi's release, but stressed that the Vatican had faith in the inherent justice of the Korean judicial process and expected that Chi's case would be fairly reviewed.

By early 1975, there was hope that Bishop Chi would be amnestied, especially since he had been charged for violating emergency degrees that had subsequently been withdrawn. The GORK did offer him release on health grounds, as the Vatican had suggested, but he refused. Chi was eventually freed and he returned to the running of his diocese.

In the wake of the fall of Saigon I requested through Archbishop Benelli that the Vatican do whatever it could to give refuge to the Koreans stranded in Saigon. Benelli promised to do whatever he could but noted that Nuncio Lemaitre in Saigon had been completely incommunicado since the fall of Saigon. Two weeks later, Benelli advised me that the Vatican had intervened on behalf of the Koreans with France and two other European governments still having missions in Saigon. These countries were all quite willing to help the Koreans but the new South Vietnamese regime had made it known that they do not recognize the right of asylum in diplomatic missions.

WESTERN EUROPE

Spain

Despite his conservative position on a number of theological issues, Pope Paul was generally a man of considerably liberal views. Politically, he would certainly have been comfortable with most social-democratic policies. He saw the problems inherent in an unbridled play of market capitalism and would certainly not have been surprised at the trouble and abuses unleashed in the 2008 worldwide financial crisis. He also saw the problems with authoritarian dictatorships. Thus, Spain was of great concern to the Vatican in the twilight years of the Franco regime. Pope Paul had inherited a Spanish hierarchy that mirrored in religious terms the deep reaction of the Franco Government. Franco was very pleased that the Spanish Church worked almost hand-in-glove with his government and did not find much to disagree with on its policies. It seems that throughout Spanish history, the Church and state worked in close cooperation to achieve mutually supportive goals.

No country considered itself closer to Rome than did Spain and no country caused so much hand-ringing in the Vatican than did Spain following the liberalization undertaken by Vatican II. Since the reign of Philip II in the 16th century, Spain fancied itself the *Espada de Roma, Luz de Trento y Martillo de Herejes* (Sword of Rome, Light of Trento, Hammer of Heretics). This outlook, if anything, was strengthened during the Franco regime. A man who most clearly epitomized this concept of Catholic Spain was Cardinal Pedro Segura, Archbishop of Seville in the pre-war period. Segura frequently warned his countrymen of the grave dangers inherent in the growing number of heretical tourists visiting Spain and advised his flock to be circumspect in their dealings with these dangerous aliens. When a defense agreement was signed between Spain and the United States in 1953, Segura was terrified about the potential for contacts between American Protestants and Spaniards. Occasionally, he even spoke fondly of the glorious days of the Inquisition that had done such a sterling job of keeping Spain free of deviation and heresy. Today, Segura would be considered something of a Catholic Wahabi.

Hidden American intentions were suspected when conservative Nevada Senator Pat McCarran visited Spain on a good-will mission. To make a favorable impression, the good senator had the crossed flags of the United States and Spain painted on the side of his official aircraft. To the horror of his Spanish hosts, the painter had used the taboo flag of the Spanish Republic instead of the Franco flag.

Under Pope Paul's leadership, the Vatican had struggled long and hard to make the Spanish hierarchy more liberal and modern. In this effort they had achieved considerable success. However, the proposal of liberal candidates to vacancies in the Spanish dioceses was a thorn in the side of Franco. He fancied himself a model Catholic and did not enjoy doing anything that placed him in disaccord with the Vatican. Moreover, as Spanish chief-of-state under the concordat that governed church-state relations, he had the right to play a major and decisive role in the choosing of candidates to fill vacancies in the ranks of the Spanish Church hierarchy. The established practice under the Concordat between Spain and the Holy See was for the Vatican and the state to produce a list of three acceptable candidates for any vacancy and for the Pope to choose one of those three. Pope Paul found himself in the unenviable position of receiving from the Government of Spain lists which contained, for him, three unacceptable choices. How to overcome this seemingly insurmountable conundrum? The Pope decided that, rather than continuing the constant and aimless bickering with the Spaniards, he would fill the vacancies with apostolic administrators rather than full residential bishops. An apostolic administrator has all the spiritual authority of a residential bishop but not the same hierarchical standing or, if you will, prestige. This practice was clearly a slap in Franco's face. After a while though, Franco gradually and quietly admitted defeat and cooperated more with the Vatican on allowing the Pope to choose his own men. Little by little and over not too many years, the Vatican managed to reorient the Spanish Church onto a much more liberal path. By the time of Franco's death, the Spanish public was gradually coming to realize that a new situation had developed, quite unlike the previous historical reality of a reactionary Church working closely with a repressive government. Remarkably, the Church had changed its spots in Spain and was no longer the archenemy of the people in league with a reactionary state. Sadly, this great and positive achievement was largely undone during the pontificate of John Paul II.

A major impediment to improved relations between the Vatican and Spain was the anachronistic Concordat of 1953, which gave vast powers to the Spanish Government in the naming of new bishops. This was a hangover from centuries before and was a practice that had long since disappeared from the Church's relations with other countries. I wondered how it had been possible even in 1953 for Spain to achieve such powers. I found the answer through my excellent contact, Monsignor José Laboa, a very well placed-Spanish liberal in the Roman Curia. Laboa, who later gained notoriety by giving temporary asylum to President Manuel Noriega of Panama when the United States ousted him in 1989. Laboa had been a young diplomat in the Papal Nunciature in Madrid when the concordat was negotiated. Laboa's boss, Nuncio and later Cardinal Gaetano Cicognani, told Laboa, as late as May 1953, that there was absolutely no possibility of signing the unacceptable draft concordat. It was signed in August! Cicognani told Laboa that pressure from the United States Government and the American Church, probably from Cardinal Francis Spellman of New York, had led Pope Pius XII to break down and accept the Spanish demands in order to facilitate the signature of our defense treaty, which followed shortly after the signing of the concordat. When I observed to Laboa that this seemed a startling involvement in church-state relations for the United States, Laboa replied that, startling or not, it was nevertheless true. The deal was easier to arrange because Cicognani's brother Amleto was at the time Apostolic Delegate in Washington where his contacts served him well.

Benelli had observed to me that a few years earlier, relations with Spain had deteriorated to such a low level that it was almost impossible to reach agreement on the appointment of any new bishops. There were at one time twenty vacancies. No candidates acceptable to the Spanish Government could be found who were also acceptable to the Holy See. At this point, the Pope, considering the situation critical, took the unusual step of writing a personal letter to General Franco asking him to relinquish Spain's traditional role in the naming of bishops. Apparently, writing to Franco was particularly galling to the Pope. Franco replied that he could not comply but suggested as an alternative that negotiations be undertaken to revise the 1953 Concordat. I then asked Benelli why an obviously unacceptable "pre-draft" of a new concordat had been circulated in Madrid. He admitted that this was difficult to explain, but felt that it was probably done as a trial balloon, which in being rejected by the Vatican and the majority of the Spanish Council of Bishops would demonstrate, to the Spanish Government that they had no case for continuing their historic involvement in Church affairs.

From talks with the Spanish Embassy to the Holy See, journalists, and some lower Vatican officials, I got the definite impression that discussions on a new concordat were quiescent. The Vatican was completely unwilling to consider a new document unless Spain fully relinquished its role in the selection of bishops. Although certain influential conservatives like Cardinal Ildebrando Antonuitti were anxious to preserve traditional Church-state links as they existed in Spain, there was virtually no likelihood that such ideas could prevail, for the Pope staunchly believed in the principles of separation developed during Vatican II. The local prognosis was that negotiations would continue spasmodically for at least another year before any genuine breakthrough occurred. The strongest desire in Rome was to continue preparing for a new-look Church in Spain that could flourish in a democratic post-Franco country.

Given the clear elevation in prestige that Pope John Paul II gave to the Opus Dei, it is hard to believe that when I was in the Vatican this controversial organization was generally considered somewhat suspect in the Curia. At the time, the Vatican was known to have been unhappy with the presence of Opus Dei in Spanish political life. There were rather creditable stories that then Secretary of State Cardinal Amleto Cicognani had, in 1964, delivered a message to General Franco from Pope Paul VI saying that he should not name Opus members to his cabinet. In the Vatican seemed to be uncomfortable with the Opus Dei both because of the organization's notorious secrecy and because the Vatican did not feel that they had sufficient authority over Opus Dei and its activities. There were also many stories about friction between Opus Dei and the Jesuit Order. Furthermore, the Church opposed the participation of clergy in political activities in any country, and clearly Opus Dei went against this policy. Moreover, their political positions were not acceptably liberal in Vatican eyes; essentially they did not support the spirit of Vatican II. Opus Dei was seen as participating with the Franco Government in crushing values that the Church revered. With hindsight, I regret not having been able to get to know such an important figure as the founder of the Opus Dei, Monsignor Escrivá de Balaguer, who lived at Opus headquarters in Rome, but given the Vatican's highly negative attitude toward him I decided it was more prudent to remain aloof.

Indeed Franco continued to provide much for us to report on. When Monsignor Laboa came back to Rome following his 1972 Christmas holiday, he told me that liberal circles in Spain were outraged over a speech by American Ambassador Rivero who had gone out of his way to praise the Franco Government. How strange, he observed, that when everyone else is abandoning Franco, the American ambassador is one of the few people to defend him. One well-placed Spanish Embassy contact told me in late 1970 that the Nixon visit to Spain had been a great mistake, especially since the survival of Francoism depended on two things: the support of the Church and the support of the United States Government. In the eyes of an ever-larger segment of the Spanish population, the Spanish Government had lost the support of the Church. On the other hand, and regrettably, the Nixon visit was viewed as an excessive act of legitimization for Franco. Whereas the Church was gaining respect for its increasing liberalization and anti-Franco posture, the United States was losing support.

In his address at the canonization of Spanish saint Teresa de Jesus Jornet Ibars on January 27, 1974, the Pope quoted Isaiah, Chapter 58, Verses 6-11, which reads, "Open your unjust prisons and free the detained. Break the chains of oppression." Reportedly, the Spanish officials attending, including Minister of Agriculture Allende, did not miss the point.

The Spanish Ambassador during most of my tour was Antonio Garrigues, a highly professional and outstanding figure of liberal and democratic sentiments in trying to steer his government along a more sensible path in their troubled dealings with the Holy See. Garrigues frequently attended lengthy and at times not terribly engaging lectures at a variety of Vatican venues. With his senior rank, he as often as not was seated in the front row of any gathering. One evening I asked him how he managed to attend so many heavy lectures, sitting bolt upright in the front row and always looking deeply absorbed and with a pleasant expression on his face. He said, "I sleep." He explained that he had long ago mastered the art of sleeping with his eyes slightly open and with an interested expression on his face. This was assuredly a rare and valuable diplomatic skill and one that on many occasions I envied not having acquired.

Portugal

The wars raging in the Portuguese colonies also provided a fertile area for political reporting. As was the case in Spain, in Portugal the Vatican was keenly aware that the Church had sadly earned a reputation as the handmaiden of the Salazar dictatorship. Salazar's early schooling in seminaries implanted in him the character of a Portuguese village priest, and throughout his entire tenure, he was closely allied with the Church. One of his closest friends and collaborators was the arch-reactionary Cardinal Manuel Cerejeira, the Patriarch of Lisbon, a man he had known since his school days. Given the fate of the African colonies of great powers like France and Great Britain, it was inconceivable that the Portuguese could manage to buck the tide of history and maintain their control in Africa. Subterfuges, like the designation of the Portuguese overseas territories as provinces on the same basis as in the metropolis, fooled no one. The Vatican expressed to me that they considered it pure folly for Portugal to resist the forces of history and try to convince the world that they had decent and workable policies in Africa. The African colonies were quite simply oppressed.

Already in 1973, Monsignor Mario Pio Gaspari expressed doubts to me about the Portuguese Government's willingness to consider any significant policy changes for their territories, particularly in matters of greater local autonomy, not to mention anything approaching independence. Any dialogue between the Portuguese Government and the Holy See was proving extremely difficult. In Gaspari's eyes, Portuguese African policy and claims of biracialism were mere propaganda and a smokescreen behind which Africans had virtually no possibility of assuming a reasonable position in society and certainly no chance of attaining meaningful positions of leadership. The school system and stringent rules for integration managed to exclude most Africans from achieving full citizenship status, he said.

The Vatican took eight months before speaking out to condemn the Portuguese massacre of civilians at Tete in December 1972. During this lapse of time, they investigated the stories of the massacre fully until they had no doubts about the terrible nature of this atrocity. Once again, Gaspari expressed to me the Vatican's failure to understand the logic of a small and poor country like Portugal squandering its limited material and human resources in a futile attempt to maintain its position in Africa when both history and local African sentiment would seem to guarantee their eventual failure. In his opinion, part of the problem was that Portugal lived in its own shell, long isolated from the main currents of thought in Europe. He felt that Portugal should both attempt to organize some sort of commonwealth with their African territories and also develop ties with the European Community. Europe could then aid in the industrialization of mainland Portugal. He suggested that NATO could encourage Portugal along these lines.

In order to position itself for a future without Portugal in Africa, the Vatican had been trying with only limited success to place more liberal bishops in African dioceses as they became vacant. A sincere effort was made to find men who were known to be sympathetic to the aspirations of the Africans. The Vatican had placed a moderately liberal man, Cardinal Patriarch Antonio Ribeiro, in Lisbon, but was rather disappointed with his lack of zeal in taking progressive initiatives. In the Vatican's eyes, many of the bishops in mainland Portugal and the colonies were poor raw material for making changes.

When Assistant Secretary of State David Newsom held discussions at the Vatican in November 1973, he noted that the United States Government had long been attempting to get the Portuguese to sit down with the Africans to work out some sort of compromise solution to their long-standing difficulties. Newsom noted that as the only country that had facilitated our resupplying of Israel, in order to maintain the military balance in the Middle East, Portugal expected us to be more understanding toward its problems in Africa.

Following the April 25, 1974 Revolution in Portugal, the Vatican was convinced that Portugal was in no way either prepared or able to continue the military fight in its African colonies. The Vatican was counselling moderation in their demands to all involved parties, seeking to get a dialogue going between Portugal and the Africans. The Portuguese Embassy to the Holy See informed me that in general they noticed a ground swell improvement in their relations with the Vatican following the April coup. The previous Ambassador Eduardo Brazão had been treated coolly, while his replacement José Calvet de Magalhães was received like a long-lost brother.

In early 1975, Casaroli expressed to me his concern for the political situation in Portugal and his fears that the elections scheduled for April may not be run honestly. The communists were well-funded from abroad and might foment some nasty actions, as was the case in Oporto. Notwithstanding, he was convinced that free elections would guarantee a victory to moderate parties. The Church would like to help, but he regretted that the Portuguese Church had had no time to remake its tarnished image as a partner with the dictatorship and thus could not really make a very positive contribution to the immediate future of the country. This situation was very different from that prevailing in Spain. Casaroli characterized Cardinal Antonio Ribeiro as very prudent in politics, but a man who "may not have the broadest political vision."

During the period of political turmoil following the April 25 Revolution up to my departure in the summer of 1975, I was able to provide a number of interesting reports on the Portuguese political situation based on information I obtained from Casaroli and Portuguese Ambassador Calvet de Magalhães. The ambassador reported that a number of his sources had mentioned that the communist parties of a number of bloc countries were distressed over the excessive zeal of the Portuguese Communist Party (PCP). It appeared that the Soviets might have come to realize that they were following mutually contradictory policies: supporting the PCP but not wishing them to take over Portugal. This was later revealed to have been true. According to Calvet de Magalhães, one of the mysteries of the Portuguese situation was that such delicate economic circumstances had not been reflected in a decline of the escudo. He attributed this to heavy secret purchases by the Soviets on the open market.

Italy

In spite of the fact that the Vatican was physically surrounded by Italy and had virtually its strongest ties with Italy, our reporting on that country was very minimal. It was apparent that the Vatican was considerably disenchanted with the Italian Church's leadership in implementing post-Vatican II policies. One bellwether question was the long time necessary to set up a justice and peace commission in Italy. In fact, Italy was by far the last European country to do so. Once it was established it showed itself to be ineffectual with an ailing and aged prelate named to the crucial position of secretary. Other European Catholic leaders were very critical of the Pope and the Italian Church over these matters. A top Vatican figure told me that the role of the Italian Church had been shocking and totally out of keeping with the Vatican's instruction to the international Church. He alleged three reasons for this: the Italian bishops had no self-consciousness and were used to being dominated by the Pope; in general and on social questions in particular the Italian bishops follow the lead of the Holy See and take no initiatives; on international questions the bishops do not even conceive that the Italian faithful have any concern or role to play. In addition to their criticisms of the Italian bishops, the Vatican was disillusioned with what had become of the Christian Democratic Party.

The depressing state of Italian political culture and the high level of corruption in Italy were common subjects of conversation in Vatican circles. One highly placed and informed journalist lamented to me that the problem was the low moral caliber of Italy's political leadership, with the possible exception of Ugo La Malfa and his Republican Party. High life and mistresses were a standard diet from the Communists through the Christian Democrats. Only Colombo and Moro were exceptions with their aesthetic life styles. In all this chaos, the Church was hoping against hope that the Christian Democrats could reform themselves, knowing full well that this was virtually impossible for a party that had been on the top for so many years. This source suspected that the United States was rapidly becoming disenchanted with their Italian counterparts and were fed up with seeing the misappropriation of American military assistance. For example, a recent study had shown that the Italian Army had a general and a colonel for each 137 soldiers, and if all the generals on active duty were put end to end the whole length of Italy, they would be spaced only 11 kilometers apart.

The above source also noted that the strength of the Mafia had reached startling proportions in Italy and, with the migration of southern Italians to northern Italy, had spread throughout the entire country for the first time. The result was that the Mafia was no doubt stronger in Milan than in Sicily. Any attempt to get at the top Mafia leadership would seem highly unlikely since the Christian Democratic Party was too intimately involved with and dependent on the Mafia for support in many areas of the South. Interior Minister Restivo was known to be thoroughly integrated into the Mafia apparatus and it was unthinkable that he would take serious measures to curb their organization. The new Archbishop of Palermo, Salvatore Pappalardo, whom the Vatican had picked to work against the Mafia, was being badly received by local power structures that were intimately involved with the Mafia. These people strongly resented the Vatican's gesture to keep the Church in Sicily away from Mafia tutelage. Pappalardo's predecessor, the late Cardinal Ruffini, although from Mantua in the North, had developed strong ties with the Mafia even before coming to Sicily.

Malta

The Archbishop of Malta, Michele Gonzi, was in his late 80s when I arrived in Rome. The Vatican had occasionally considered trying to seek his retirement, especially since he was far past the normal age (75) to resign his diocese, and moreover was very deaf and becoming less mentally agile. Gonzi, unlike his deputy Bishop Emanuele Gerada, was not considered to be on the best of terms with the Socialist leader Dom Mintoff, although by 1974 their relationship had improved greatly. I followed the vicissitudes of the Gonzi saga and also the approach to the close elections of 1971.

As the British were in the process of winding down their long-standing military and naval presence in Malta, the question was open as to whom, if anyone, would replace them. There was concern that Colonel Gaddafi of Libya was willing to make up for the damaging financial loss that a British departure would inflict on the Maltese economy in exchange for increased influence and military rights. Given Mintoff's leftist leanings, there was also concern that he might open Malta to a presence from the Soviet Bloc. My contacts in the Order of Malta believed that at this time it was important for the United States Government to make some sort of approach to Mintoff, who had in fact won the 1971 elections. The Knights, who tended to have excellent contacts in the Maltese Government, informed me that Mintoff would look favorably to an opening from the United States.

On January 27, 1972, Benelli called me urgently to his office to show me a letter he had received the previous evening from Archbishop Gonzi. The letter reported on a long talk the Archbishop had just had with Mintoff, in which Mintoff expressed his willingness to accept an offer of a UK-NATO agreement of a seven-year base agreement for 14 million pounds. The clincher was that he also needed an additional one-time supplementary payment of 10.5 million pounds. In his letter, Gonzi made an impassioned plea for the Pope to intervene with President Nixon in the hope that Mintoff's demands might be met. Benelli told me that, of course, the Holy See was unable to judge the real worth of Malta to the Allies in military terms, but he was very hopeful that some sort of agreement could be reached. The Vatican did share Gonzi's fear that if the British left, another power would certainly fill the vacuum, probably not Soviets themselves, but most likely someone not friendly to the West. He asked that this message, which was only being discussed with us, be kept secret, as the Vatican would not like to be seen as acting in anything approaching an intermediary capacity in this context. The Knights of Malta also informed me that they knew of Mintoff's desire for a deal involving the United States Government. The Order's ambassador in Malta, Marrajeni, was one of the few foreigners to have close relations with Mintoff, who had confided to him on the foregoing.

An amusing sideline of the above was the fact that the Order of Malta had been negotiating for some time with Malta to obtain a sliver of land or even a tiny island off the Maltese coast to use as a base from which to establish their sovereignty in a meaningful sense. The Knights had been headquartered in Rome since 1834, but only had what in reality amounted to extraterritorial status. The problem at the time was that the order had high hopes of being permitted to use their postage stamps internationally. This would provide them a heightened source of much-needed revenue to carry out their vast array of medical and charitable activities. The stamps would only be accepted by the Universal Postal Union, however, if they were issued by an entity with genuine sovereignty.

Mintoff visited the Vatican in August 1974 to discuss planned changes in the Maltese Constitution. He found the

Vatican totally understanding with his intent to remove language giving certain specified rights to the Catholic Church, although a statement that Catholicism was the official religion of the state would be maintained for the present. The Vatican informed him that they had no difficulty with the proposed changes, which in any case reflected the philosophy of the separation of state and church embodied in the reforms of Vatican II.

Northern Ireland

Conquered at the close of the 12th century during the reign of King John, Ireland can easily be considered the first colony of a European country. Although England and Ireland shared the Catholic faith for the first 350 years of their relationship, the English undertook immediately a process of colonizing Ireland with Englishmen and generally reduced the native Irish population to the status of second-class citizens. The status of the native Irish was further negatively impacted by the Protestant Reformation, during which the bulk of the Anglo-Irish adopted the new faith and the native Irish remained loyal to the Church of Rome. The creation of the Irish Republic after World War I did not ease the situation in what became Northern Ireland, a festering sore in the British body politic until it exploded in the 1960s.

Beyond counselling moderation, the Vatican bent over backwards to maintain a neutral stand on the question of Northern Ireland, scrupulously avoiding efforts to convince them to take sides. Although he was sensitive to the Vatican's position, Irish Ambassador Thomas Commins was instructed in February 1972 to make a request for the Vatican's support on the following three points: total withdrawal of British troops from Ulster; end of the policy of internment without trial; and convocation of a conference to settle the future of Ulster. Casaroli rejected a Vatican role on these three points as they all were of a definitely political nature which the Vatican had neither legitimate concern nor ability to evaluate.

Shortly after this request from Ireland, British Minister to the Holy See Desmond Crawley asked the Vatican to use its influence to have a mass march cancelled. In this case, Casaroli

did agree to ask the Catholic hierarchy in the North to do everything reasonably possible to exert a modifying influence on the
participants. When Prime Minister Edward Heath met with the
Pope on October 4, 1972, the Pope expressed understanding for
British efforts to achieve a peaceful solution to the Ulster crisis,
but he also expressed concern over the continuing British policy
of internment.

Later in November 1974, the desk officer for Great Britain
told me that the Vatican was deeply unhappy over the British
use of torture in Ulster. When I asked him just what he meant
by torture, he admitted that it was normally not of the sadistic
kind but did include beating and kicking young Catholic youths
by heavily shod soldiers and dragging boys about by their hair.
He also felt that the application of curfew rules was ridiculously
strict, with large numbers of 14–15-year-old youths being arrested
moments after the curfew began and being placed in internment
camps where they were brutally treated and groundlessly accused
of being terrorists. Catholic chaplains in the British Army also
intimidated detained Irish Catholic youths. Only when the Head
Army Chaplain in London took an interest in the matter did
this type of harassment cease. Of course, all of this harshness was
counterproductive, tending to radicalize young men and drive
them into the camp of the extremists.

Eastern Europe and Vatican Ostpolitik

Without doubt, no area gave more urgent concern to
the Vatican than did the nations of Eastern Europe, especially
the countries with Catholic majorities like Poland, Hungary,
and Czechoslovakia. With officially atheistic ideologies, these
communist regimes put as many obstacles in the way of the
free exercise of religion as they could. In the case of Poland,
the communists had to tread notably more lightly due to the
public's overwhelmingly strong loyalty to the Church. The
Polish Government's relations with the Vatican blew hot and
cool, and when I was there, the Vatican was deeply engaged in
their *Ostpolitik*, or new policies, to seek expanded and improved
relations with communist Eastern Europe. Much of this new trend

was undertaken in the spirit of the Conference of Security and Cooperation in Europe (CSCE) in which the Holy See was fully and enthusiastically participating. Receptivity on the communist sides was determined by a number of factors: the degree of official liberalization at the time, including often the degree of liberalism of an individual functionary in charge of church-state relations; the public mood; and last but not least, the state of pressure from the Soviet Union and the length to which local governments were prepared to go to stand up to their Soviet overlords. As a result, the state of play of state-church relations was a good barometer of the general trends in local ideological politics. Our reporting to our embassies in the bloc countries provided very useful information and insights into the state of Vatican activities in the various communist countries.

Following the example of the Western democracies, the Holy See had embarked on a series of efforts to mend its eastern fences, hoping thereby to improve the lot of Catholics living under communist rule. Within these countries, any minor gains in religious freedom had usually resulted from general improvements in domestic social and political conditions. In certain instances, the continued resistance and courage of the local Catholic leadership had, to some limited extent, been able to win concessions from reluctant civil authorities. Also, a number of leaders had come to realize that continued implacable hostility toward religion was often counterproductive, and that a somewhat more nuanced and conciliatory approach might in fact help to brighten the regimes' usually tarnished images.

The Vatican's approach to the communist world seemed grounded on certain basic principles and assumptions. Of prime importance was the firm conviction that religious freedom was a root or germinal freedom. Once a communist regime had allowed even a slight improvement in the lot of believers, it had allowed the seeds of questioning and doubt to be sowed in its citizens' minds. Having savored some religious liberty, the believer's appetite was inevitably whetted for other liberties. This reasoning seemed to discount the attitude of many former Christian sovereigns toward freedom, especially Byzantium, Russia, and other eastern lands.

163

Nonetheless, the political liberals who controlled Vatican relations with the communist world did expound and most likely believe this principle.

Another guiding principle was that Eastern Europe was a reservoir of great spirituality, an area that in many ways had escaped the corrosive influences of modern affluent society. Some churchmen would even maintain that the harsh communist life had been a crucible purifying man for a religious revival, in a sense a baptism of fire. This argument, although having opposite causes, is not unlike the theory attributing the increased spirituality of American youth to a reaction against a surfeit of wealth and plenty.

In Vatican estimates, programs to inculcate atheism in Eastern Europe had failed. The masses remained strongly religious, and the youth were experiencing a measurable increase in religiosity following years of apathy and hostility. Recognizing the failure of their atheistic policies, communist regimes, or so believed the Vatican, were sometimes begrudgingly willing to grant some increase in religious freedom. Obviously the regime had the upper hand, withdrawing concessions when it believed the situation had gone too far. In spite of this, the Church felt that once a communist regime had made even minor concessions, it had helped sow the seeds of its own eventual destruction or liberalization. In this light, the regimes often unwittingly made what could eventually develop into major concessions.

For its own survival in a recognizable form, the Catholic Church sought to achieve certain concrete goals in communist dominated areas. One goal was, of course, to rebuild its sorely decimated hierarchical structures. Only a properly chosen and installed bishop could give the necessary prestige and authority to a diocese, not to mention the important sacramental functions which only he could perform. A second goal was to establish full communications with the Vatican, at a minimum through the free exchange of persons and correspondence, and ideally with the opening of a Vatican diplomatic mission in the foreign capital. The third desideratum was to guarantee greater freedom for Church operations and the exercise of religion by the faithful.

The Vatican's main technique for achieving the above had been through the exchange of visits and personal meetings with both religious and civil leaders. The Church was clearly convinced that all contacts were useful and little by little might have some salutary influence on the communist leaders. The Vatican also believed that it could maintain firm control of any negotiations with communist officials, always coming out ahead in an eventual agreement. God, time. and justice were on the Church's side, and His truth was infectious, always prevailing in the end. Therefore, the Vatican put great store in the ecumenical movement, which placed churchmen from totalitarian countries in close contact with their free world counterparts. As the oldest diplomatic practitioner, the Vatican sincerely believed it could maintain the advantage in dealing with atheist adversaries.

The Vatican's foreign minister, Archbishop Agostino Casaroli, properly titled Secretary of the Council for Public Affairs of the Church, supervised overall policy with the communist countries. His principal deputy was Monsignor Giovanni Cheli, the astute Italian who resolved the perennial Mindszenty case. Formally, Cheli was responsible for Czechoslovakia, Hungary, and Romania. Monsignor Gabriel Montalvo, a Colombian son of a former Colombian Ambassador to the Holy See, handled Bulgaria, Poland, and the Soviet Union. Since Montalvo's experience and probably also expertise was limited, Cheli in fact handled all significant matters at the working level. Another Italian, Monsignor Angelo Sodano, completed the Eastern European division. Cardinal Franz König of Vienna, who was often considered the "Vatican's Eastern European expert," in reality never acted as a representative of the Holy See. As the spiritual leader of a neighboring country with historical ties to the East, it was natural for him to take a special interest in Eastern Europe. His role, however, was largely ceremonial, or based on his personal interests. According to reliable Vatican sources, he never carried out missions, sensitive or otherwise. Of course, this did not preclude his making delicate visits such as when he called on Cardinal Mindszenty, who incidentally was not particularly sympathetic to König, whom he considered too young and inexperienced to deal successfully with communism. Some of Casaroli's staff considered König something of a meddlesome gadfly.

At the time, the state of relations between the Vatican and Eastern Europe nations ranged from a total lack of communication with Albania to correct and full diplomatic relations with Yugoslavia. Contacts with Bulgaria and Romania, both having fairly small Catholic populations, were virtually non-existent, although Church officials occasionally visited Catholic authorities there. The *Exarch* of Sofia and the Catholic Bishop of Alba Julia were able to travel to Rome as delegates to the 1971 Synod of Bishops. Since President Podgorny's call on Pope Paul in 1967, there had been an increase in contacts with the Soviet Union, culminating with Archbishop Casaroli's dramatic visit in the spring of 1971, ostensibly to sign the Nuclear Non-Proliferation Treaty. In spite of the growing frequency of contacts, the Holy See was not sanguine about significant improvements in relations or religious liberalizations in the Soviet Union. Relations with Czechoslovakia were at a chilled impasse; hopes to continue the dialogue opened in Rome in April 1971 had been dashed by an intensified anti-religious campaign by the communist government. As predominately and strongly Catholic countries, both Poland and Hungary had rather frequent contacts with the Holy See. The role of the Church in Poland was more unassailable, but in negotiations for the departure of Cardinal Mindszenty, the Hungarians showed an increased willingness to make some compromises with the Church. The Vatican had little contact with East Germany, a primarily Protestant country. Although the status of believers in Yugoslavia was far from ideal, given present conditions and attitudes among Eastern European officials, the Vatican hoped that its achievements in Yugoslavia could serve as a model for other communist countries.

The Vatican proceeded cautiously with the communist nations and with limited short-term expectations. It harbored no illusions of rapid or dramatic success, knowing full well that the harsh communist leaders had not softened their determined opposition to religion. Nonetheless, permitting itself its habitual luxury of viewing situations with a broad historical perspective, the Vatican believed that time was on the side of religion. The failure to force atheism on Eastern Europe had occasionally led the regimes to seek certain accommodations with religious authorities. Therefore, Vatican policy makers did not want to be unreceptive to possibilities for easing religious oppression under communism. They did not see this in the context of weakened opposition to Godless Marxism, but as mindfulness of the welfare of millions of Christians living under communism. Also, the desire to make the Church worldwide an independent force, not the spokesman of one particular political ideology, should have, according to Church planners, placed it in a more favorable light to political leaders. Having cleaned house a good deal by removing some of the unattractive features of the pre-Vatican II Church, the Vatican hoped to find less opposition among leaders, even in Eastern Europe. They hoped that the relative success of the experiment in Yugoslavia would point the way for other communist countries. History bore out their wisdom!

Hungary

The ultimate departure of Cardinal Mindszenty opened a path for further improvements in relations with the Church in Hungary as his continued presence in Hungary had been a thorn in the side of the local communist leadership. Eventually full residential bishops were named to long-vacant sees and finally Mindszenty was replaced as the Archbishop of Esztegom, the main Hungarian see. Mindszenty, from his home in Vienna, expressed privately his unveiled hostility toward Archbishop Casaroli, whose role in opening relations between the Vatican and East Europe he considered sinister and replete with great disaster for the Church. In the cardinal's eyes, everything the Vatican considered advantageous in their accomplishments in Eastern Europe was damaging to the Church's long range interests.

A major unresolved problem after Mindszenty's departure was the fate of the Holy Crown of St. Stephan. This was not your typical royal crown, but was considered the vessel of Hungarian sovereignty. Whoever had physical possession of the crown was considered the legitimate ruler of Hungary. For that reason the

United States had cooperated at the end of World War II in spiriting the crown out of Hungary to the U.S., to avoid it falling into Soviet hands. On instructions from the State Department in early 1973, Lodge asked the Pope whether the Vatican wished to play a role in returning the crown to the Hungarian Government. We noted playfully that since one of the Pope's predecessors, in the year 1000, had originally given the crown to St. Stephan, King of Hungary, to symbolize his conversation to Catholicism, Pope Paul might wish to repeat the gesture. The Pope forcefully demurred. In the end, the United States returned the crown directly to the Hungarian Government.

Poland

The Vatican was able to exercise a relatively free hand in the naming of bishops to Polish dioceses with the singular exception of the territories in Western Poland that had been taken from Germany at the end of World War II. The major problem in this region was the absence of a formal peace treaty between Poland and East Germany that legitimized the new borders. The Vatican had a long-standing and well-established policy of not accepting border changes that were not recognized in a formal treaty valid under international law. Following the Federal Republic of Germany's (FRG) parliamentary resolution on the FRG-Polish treaty in June 1972, the Vatican choose to find this sufficient justification to act on the naming of full residential bishops in Western Poland.

Any hope of establishing diplomatic relations with Poland was held in abeyance until such time as a treaty might be signed. Another somewhat peculiar obstacle was that the Vatican continued to have diplomatic relations with the Polish Government in Exile (the London Government). Casimir Papée, an 85-year-old diplomat from the old regime occupied the rather curious position of *Gérant des Affaires*. Casaroli told me that he considered this more a courtesy position rather than a proper diplomatic one, the inference being that whenever the Vatican was in a position to open a nunciature in Warsaw he would not be an obstacle.

The Vatican believed that opening a nunciature in Warsaw was a two-edged sword. On the one hand, it would facilitate communications, but, on the other hand, having normalized diplomatic relations it might encourage the Polish Government to attempt to use this direct channel to the Vatican to try to marginalize the local Church. In mid-1974, the Vatican accepted a Polish plan to send three new staff members to the Polish Embassy in Rome charged with dealing exclusively with the Vatican. These three officials ended up establishing an office outside of the Polish Embassy to Italy and had no diplomatic accreditation, following the practice established by the Lodge mission. There was no immediate plan for reciprocity on the Vatican side, out of deference to the wishes of Cardinal Stefan Wyszynski, the Primate of Poland.

The Italian Embassy to the Holy See informed me that Italian Intelligence was convinced that two of the three members of the new Polish mission to the Holy See were in fact clandestine agents covering Italy. I also learned from British Intelligence sources that they knew for sure that one Iranian, one Egyptian, and two Cubans from their respective embassies to the Holy See were intelligence operatives, also concentrating mainly on Italian concerns.

When a Vatican delegation visited Poland in early 1975, several Church groups were flabbergasted to find that the Vatican had put a "Russian named Ivan" on the delegation. When they saw that the new Polish desk officer was Monsignor Ivan Dias from Bombay, they were obviously reassured. On every occasion during the visit, however, the Polish bishops referred to Dias as Ivo or Jan, but never Ivan, his real name. A bit provincial perhaps!

Czechoslovakia

Although communications with the Church in Czechoslovakia were reasonably good, the Vatican's relationship with the government was poor. The climate was cold and the infrequent contacts were conducted in an atmosphere verging on open hostility. The Vatican believed that the leadership realized that the population was thirsting for the liberties they had briefly acquired under former president Aleksander Dubcek, and therefore felt constrained to give a little in some areas, including religious freedom. The Vatican had to wait very patiently for these hopes to be fulfilled.

In 1974, Monsignor Cheli, the Vatican's negotiator for Eastern Europe, considered the situation worse than in the time of former hard-line President Novotny just prior to 1968. He admitted though that the situation looked much better on paper than in reality, especially since legislation was more liberal and famous show trials of churchmen no longer took place. However, Cheli saw the state using much more sophisticated and insidious techniques to attack the Church. For example, in 1971, the Czech Government had initiated a determined campaign to force older priests and religious into retirement. These retirements were achieved through simple administrative procedures such as the withdrawal of work permits. Those few priests who had appealed to the authorities found all avenues for reversal of these administrative decisions blocked. In addition, many priests had had their work permits administratively withdrawn as a result of trumped up charges of legal violations. Cheli found it particularly agonizing to deal with Karel Hruza, the official in charge of religious affairs. Hruza from time to time suggested to Cheli that the question of the vacant dioceses be settled, but it quickly became apparent that his ideas of how to settle this long-standing grievance were totally unacceptable to the Church. Hruza was wrong, Cheli said, in his belief that the Vatican was desperate to fill these vacancies in any manner due to the long time they had been vacant.

Cheli favored a hard-line approach toward the Czechs, which by 1972 he felt was losing favor with many of his colleagues in the Curia, including probably the Pope. This distressed him deeply, as he was firmly convinced that the hard-line was giving the Eastern Europeans the impression that the Vatican meant business and was a formidable adversary. When Cheli visited Hong Kong and Macau in late 1972, Casaroli requested Radio Free Europe to announce this mission in the hope that Eastern Europeans might get a little worried to think that Vatican feelers might be going out to Communist China. The broadcast must have made some impact in Prague because, when greeting Cheli on his next visit to

Prague, Hruza asked him casually how he enjoyed his recent visit to see Mao. Cheli came to believe that the Czech Government was a particularly odious government doing everything in its power to make itself even more odious to the people. He considered them without question the most blatantly atheistic government among the satellites.

On March 4, the Pope announced that he had chosen Bishop Stepán Trochta of Litomerice to be a cardinal. Casaroli and Cheli were in Prague at the time and decided to inform the Czechs only the evening before so that the Czech Government would have no time to block the announcement in Rome the following day. Deputy Premier Lucan protested the manner in which the announcement was made, but did not comment on the choice of Trochta whom, Cheli noted to me, was the bishop least acceptable to the government due to his firmness. Sadly, Cardinal Trochta died just one year later.

While sitting in Archbishop Benelli's waiting room in March 1971, I met Cardinal Wojtyla, who also had an appointment with Benelli. I was able to have a pleasant one-hour chat with him, first in his excellent Italian and then, when a Canadian cardinal came into the room, in tolerably good English. Regrettably, we had to cut short our interesting conversation to non-political matters. Cardinal Wojtyla felt that the current situation with more frequent talks between Poland and the Vatican hopefully presented certain opportunities for the Church to improve its status. He noted, however, that the Soviet Union was suspicious of an international religion like Catholicism—a heritage from czarist times—and would urge its satellites to progress slowly in dealing with the Vatican. The Vatican leadership, he pointed out, was well aware of these traditional Russian concerns.

Soviet Union

The Vatican did have occasional limited contacts with the Soviet Embassy to Italy. Casaroli had held discussions with Soviet Ambassador Ryzhov for more important matters and Monsignor Montalvo periodically had chats of a more general nature with Soviet First Secretary Igor Saudarev. Montalvo was Soudarev's only contact at the Vatican and wide-ranging talks covered such areas as the Middle East, Church problems in Spain and Holland, and Latin America. Montalvo told me that Soudarev never told him anything of consequence. Saudarev invariably refused to give a meaningful answer to any question that Montalvo posed.

A sticking point between the Soviet Union and the Catholic Church was the existence of the Ukrainian Uniate Church, which in spite of its Orthodox traditions and rites, recognized the authority of the Pope in Rome. This Church was created in the 16th century at a time when Western Ukraine was under Polish rule. To further aggravate an already tense situation, Stalin had imprisoned the head of the Ukrainian Uniate Church, Cardinal Josyf Slipyj, for anti-Soviet activities. Slipyj remained in prison for 18 years until Norman Cousins and Nikita Khrushchev negotiated his release in 1963. Slipyj was a remarkable man whose mind and body remained unbroken throughout his long incarceration. When I knew him in Rome, he was in his early 90s, a tall, rigid figure who stood out dramatically in Vatican processions with his high white Orthodox hat. The Soviets in general considered the Uniate Church to be a relic of Western Christian and Polish imperialism and had confiscated its property.

Yugoslavia

Considering it was a communist country, relations with the Church in Yugoslavia could be generally characterized as satisfactory. There were diplomatic relations and President Tito had made a state visit to the Vatican in 1971. When Casaroli met with Tito in September 1970, an interesting dialogue ensued. He told the President that the whole nonalignment movement was aimlessly bogged down in negativism and polemics excoriating the alleged "imperialists" for all the world's ills. He warned Tito that nonalignment, a potential for good and a useful forum for smaller and developing countries, was dissipating its energy in counterproductive attacks against those countries which in reality were best able to help them in a positive way. It would be better, he told Tito, if the nonaligned would devote themselves to constructive criticisms and establish concrete proposals for improving the world situation. Otherwise, the whole movement would become ridiculous. Casaroli noted that the so-called superpowers were a reality, and whatever good developed in the world would in great part depend on them, as would the bad. It was inevitable, Casaroli warned Tito, that the nonaligned must cooperate with the great powers if they really wished to achieve the noble objectives embodied in their principles. Casaroli said that Tito listened with interest, and at the end commented that it was true no lasting solutions for world problems could be achieved by the nonaligned alone, but that cooperation must be sought with the great powers.

On March 29, 1971, President Tito became the first communist chief-of-state to pay a formal visit on the Pope. Resplendent in white tie, silk top hat and decorations, Tito and party—ladies all in full length black dresses and long mantillas—received full honors including the playing of the Yugoslav national anthem by the Pontifical Band while Yugoslav flags fluttered from the Apostolic Palace. The Pope and Tito spoke alone with interpreters for 75 minutes. According to Vatican sources, nothing particularly surprising or interesting was discussed during the private talks which covered the Middle East, Vietnam, racism in Southern Africa, and development. In a warm statement he made following the audience, Tito noted with pleasure that the "Holy See and Yugoslavia had similar or identical views on major international problems."

A member of the Pope's household told me an amusing story after the Tito visit. He said everyone was expecting to see a tough, robust-looking character walk in, especially after hearing all the stories of Tito's herculean exploits during the war. Instead, many were surprised and somewhat disappointed when a mild-looking, little old man showed up, full of reverence and rather subdued. I told him he should not be deceived by appearances, as Tito still seemed to have a lot of fire left in him.

LATIN AMERICA

Although Latin American was beyond a doubt the most solidly Catholic continent on the globe, it surprisingly generated less reporting for us than many other areas. This was due in great part to the fact that the Vatican did not suffer some of the same disabilities in the area that they suffered, for example, in the bloc countries. The Church was basically free to name whomever they wished to vacant dioceses and to maintain normal communications with the leaders of the local Churches. However, satisfactory relationships on the purely ecclesiastical level often did not guarantee good political relationships with the harsh and oppressive dictatorships in Latin America. In countries like Nicaragua, El Salvador, Brazil, Argentina, and Chile, the Church was often the only tolerated locus of opposition, or at least criticism, of the regimes. While local churchmen frequently came into conflict with the oppressive governments, the political leaders in the last analysis usually found it expedient not to go all out in attacking the Church.

Latin America, due primarily to its poverty, social injustice, lack of human rights, and its Catholic traditions, was the area in which the Justice and Peace Commissions, the Church organs to deal with these types of problems, were most engaged. The Commission in Rome felt that Latin Americans, including the elite and the masses, essentially had been practicing the same Catholicism introduced in the 16th century by Spanish missionaries. With its emphasis on fatalism in this world and man's just rewards in the afterlife, these beliefs had generally fortified the oligarchies' control over the underprivileged masses. To exacerbate the situation, rendering it even more impervious to change, many Latin Americans sincerely believed in the divinely-inspired organization of secular society into the elite and the masses. Yet in the 1970s, the masses, realizing in many cases for the first time that they were being brutally exploited, had awakened, and were no longer willing to accept unquestioningly the current social order.

Top officials of the Justice and Peace Commission in Rome saw Latin America on the threshold of massive change, which they believed no force could or should attempt to restrain. The Vatican wished to identify those forces striving for positive change within an acceptable Christian context, and to unite with them. The

Church feared abandoning the field to the prophets of atheism and violent revolution.

Monsignor Joseph Gremillion considered the Church one of the few institutions with sufficient power and influence to arouse Latin America for positive change. To do this effectively, the Church had to sincerely change its historic image. This process was already underway, especially among the younger and more altruistic clergy. Monsignor Gremillion left me no doubt that the Holy See fully endorsed the Church's role in social change, and had given approval to his Commission's undertakings aimed at carrying it out.

Chile

The Latin American country that generated the largest volume of reporting for us was unquestionably Chile, and all parties attested to the usefulness of the information and insights we obtained through our Vatican contacts. We first discussed Chile with high-level Vatican contacts on the eve of the fall 1970 election that gave the presidency to Salvador Allende. While the Vatican felt unable to affect the election outcome, it also somehow felt confident that Chilean democratic traditions would manage to moderate the worst of what many people felt were Allende's extremist ideas. The Vatican's unwillingness to take sides in the election was due considerably to respect for liberal Cardinal Raúl Silva Henríquez, Archbishop of Santiago. In general, the Vatican felt that Allende would win and that the Chileans and their Church would know best how to keep him from passing totally under communist control or from moving too far to the left.

By mid-1972, the Vatican was becoming disillusioned with events in Allende's Chile. Many contacts found Cardinal Silva, the Archbishop of Santiago, overly naïf and often in the hands of poorly-selected leftist priests. A number of contacts felt that if current trends had continued, and if Allende had made an undeniable movement toward setting up a communist dicta- torship, there was good chance of a civil war and a massive flight of the middle classes.

Following the military coup that removed Allende, one Vatican contact who looked with some favor on the military leaders was the generally liberal Provost General of the Jesuit Order, Father Pedro Arrupe. He told me that he gained from his September 1973 visit to Chile the impression that those who organized the military coup were decent people and not militaristic adventurers. Believers in democracy, they had organized the coup because they were convinced that something violent and extremely dangerous was about to happen, and which had to be forestalled before it was too late. Just after the military coup, the general impression among ranking Vatican officials with whom I spoke was that the ruling junta was composed of good men compelled to move in defense of Chilean independence and democracy only after Allende's Government had created an intolerable situation and was mortally threatened by a coup of utmost violence from the opposite end of the political spectrum. Cardinal Sebastiano Baggio, who had been Papal Nuncio in Santiago for six years, said he knew many of the junta leaders and he was convinced that they were honorable men who were motivated by sincere convictions and genuine democratic instincts. How sadly mistaken these usually astute observers were! Only "Deputy Foreign Minister" Monsignor Achille Silvestrini was more accurate when he told me that yes, they may be good men, but once having savored power it was seriously doubtful that they would soon relinquish it.

A month after the coup, Archbishop Benelli expressed to me his deep concern over the manner in which the worldwide leftist press had managed successfully to distort the situation in Chile. In reality, he believed the communists had managed to turn a defeat in Chile into a victory through their highly successful propaganda. On the basis of calming reports from Cardinal Silva and the Nunciature, the Vatican was firmly convinced that Allende was preparing a communist coup and that he had heavily armed the working class with weapons provided through the good offices of the Cuban diplomatic mission. Six months later, our Vatican contacts were convinced that a heavy-handed repression was indeed underway in Chile. By this point, the Chilean Church was contemplating ways to attack the widespread human rights violations but found it difficult to find just the right path as too much criticism could redound to the advantage of the left.

A few years before the coup, I had picked up from highly-placed Vatican officials reports that the CIA was involved in public safety programs in Latin America. On one of his visits Lodge refuted these stories, presumably to the satisfaction of the Vatican where most officials were disposed to "believe the best about the USG." In early 1974, we even considered asking the Vatican if they could lean on Chilean Church for some documentation giving us a clean bill of health for non-involvement in the overthrow of Allende. Fortunately we did not pursue this cynical project, which was geared to "dispelling the ugly rumors about our involvement."

By June 1974, the Chilean bishops had become thoroughly disenchanted with the state of human rights violations and government brutality, and they felt that they must speak out forcefully. While they understood that some turmoil might be inevitable after a coup, seven months of unrelenting horror was clearly too much. Although President Pinochet was displeased with the bishops' statement, Cardinal Silva encouraged him to accept it in a positive light, endorse it, and turn it to the government's advantage by using it as leverage to eliminate police abuses with which Pinochet himself expressed strong abhorrence to the Cardinal. At a working dinner at the Papal Nunciature in Santiago, Pinochet had told the Cardinal that he himself was deeply troubled by reports of police violence, excesses, and the use of torture. He assured Cardinal Silva that he did not sympathize with these tactics and had in fact issued stringent orders that they be halted. He was aware, however, that officials at the local level, often in areas far from Santiago, were not heeding these instructions. Cardinal Silva believed that Pinochet was sincere when he claimed he was making an attempt to restrain excesses of police and security forces. We later learned that this belief of the Cardinal's was sadly misplaced!

Paraguay

Paraguayan dictator Stroessner had an audience with Pope Paul on July 25, 1973, during which the Pope appealed to him in the strongest terms to exercise clemency toward persons detained for political crimes. Stroessner did not give the Pontiff assurances on this request, but more interestingly, neither did he deny the existence of political prisoners in Paraguay or try to define such persons as normal criminals. The Pope also explained to Stroessner that the local bishops needed more freedom to fulfil their mission. He had particularly in mind the task of local bishops to identify abuses of human rights. As a result of this visit, a total of 70 political prisoners were released, which gave the Vatican some satisfaction, although my sources admitted that they had no idea just how many political prisoners may have remained in detention.

Cuba

Following a ten-day visit to Cuba in early 1974 at the invitation of the Cuban bishops, Archbishop Casaroli told me that he had been able to travel freely throughout the country and visit all six dioceses and to meet with most of Cuba's 200-odd clergy. He said that he was warmly received wherever he went and he believed that his visit was extremely useful in pulling up the spirits of the Cuban clergy. The fact that he met with the highest levels of government, he said, also convinced Cuban Catholics that the Church still carried considerable weight in Cuba and that the government took serious notice of it. Although his visit was purely private in nature, he was surprised by the level of attention shown him by high government officials, including a meeting with Foreign Minister Roa. An additional special touch was Roa's presence at the airport on Casaroli's departure. Casaroli met with President Dorticós and, most significantly, had a 90-minute meeting with Fidel Castro. When Casaroli and the Nuncio arrived home at 11 p.m., they were surprised by a telephone call from Castro saying that he would be by in about half an hour. Castro told Casaroli that it was the government's wish that Catholics consider themselves full members of Cuban society and that, as far as he was concerned, the only thing a practicing Catholic could not do would be to become a party member. Although Castro did not say it, implicit in his remarks was the thought that Catholics were second-class citizens and had withdrawn themselves from full participation in Cuban society and had not been forced to withdraw by any pressure from the government. In response to a question from Casaroli, Roa told him that the Cuban Government would consider improved ties with the U.S. only if the U.S. lifted the embargo against Cuba.

Argentina

In late 1972, the Vatican began hearing rumors that former President Juan Perón was contemplating a trip to Rome and would be interested in having a papal audience. The Vatican was hoping to stave off any visit from Perón. Vatican officials were particularly concerned about being drawn into any action that might be interpreted as lending support to Perón. If it were to become apparent that Perón anticipated a return to Argentina, however, there was no doubt that the Vatican would grant any request from Perón for an audience. In the end Perón did come to Rome and on November 15, 1972, Casaroli met with him for 75 minutes at his hotel. Casaroli said Perón showed no bitterness that a Papal audience had not been arranged and accepted without hesitation Casaroli's explanation that the Vatican preferred not to become involved in Argentine politics at such a critical moment. Casaroli told me that an audience was never formally requested, but that when Perón's aides learned of Vatican reticence to grant an audience, they did not pursue the matter. The Vatican had, however, made it clear to Perón's aides that an audience would have been granted if they had insisted and made a formal request. Casaroli found Perón in excellent physical and mental form. Particularly impressive were the breadth of his knowledge of world affairs and his analytical powers. Casaroli told me that he could not share much of Perón's philosophy, but that Perón displayed considerable mental agility in expounding it.

AFRICA

Given the number of problems in Africa involving conflicts between prelates and the local rulers, the Vatican probably considered Africa more the red continent than the black one. In the eyes of the Vatican, most of these conflicts stemmed more from the impossibility for most African leaders to tolerate any power structure or institution not firmly under their iron-fisted control rather than from anything the Churches were actually doing in Africa. Our mission provided great assistance to the Vatican in cases where African prelates were under serious threat from local leaders. Our communications facilities, advice, and intelligence were very useful to them.

Zaire

One of the "red Africans" that gave considerable concern to the Vatican leadership was Cardinal Joseph Malula, Archbishop of Kinshasha and nominal head of the Church in Zaire. Already in 1971, President Mobutu was finding Malula an uncomfortable competitor in a world where the President was monopolizing ever more plenary and dictatorial powers. Not that Malula, a quiet man, had done anything either to upstage, or much less, threaten the President's paramount position of power; it was just the almost pervasive African situation wherein the political leader found any focus of power not totally under his control unacceptable.

At the heart of the problem was Mobutu's *authenticité* campaign in which all citizens of Zaire were required to adopt African names and to abandon ideas and practices imported by the former European colonial masters. The Church had no objection to the use of African names, provided one of a person's names, even if never used, be a Christian one. The Church did, however, worry about the possibility of a return to pagan African religious beliefs and practices. It must also be remembered that President Mobutu was at this time a practicing Catholic.

In an effort to resolve this festering conflict, Archbishop Casaroli met in Lausanne in January 1972 with President Mobutu. His message to the President was that there were many advantages to letting the Church exist as an independent but totally loyal free force within Zaire, but he was not sure that Mobutu was very sympathetic to this argument, which was seemingly difficult for a non-Westerner to understand. African leaders not only wished to *be* all-powerful; they also insisted upon *appearing* so. Casaroli had hoped subtly to demonstrate, without of course openly saying so, that Zaire could use the existence of an independent Church to refute claims of opponents attempting to demonstrate that Zaire had become a totalitarian state.

The Vatican believed that at this juncture it would be useful for the Cardinal to come to Rome for a cooling off period, but under no circumstances did they wish to oblige him to do so. They simply left the door open for him to decide. Malula was a very courageous man but not overly resourceful. The Vatican knew that if they were seen to welcome his coming to Rome this would be perceived in Zaire and elsewhere in Africa as a sign that troublesome prelates could easily be gotten rid of—with Vatican compliance.

When the Zairian Government finally gave its assurances that the Cardinal could return to Zaire, Malula decided to fly to Rome for a rest. The Vatican was shocked, however, when shortly thereafter, Mobutu announced that the Cardinal could return to Zaire "only as a private citizen." No definition of that terminology was given but the Vatican feared the worst. Even Zairian Ambassador to the Holy See Sita Pambu, who enjoyed high regard at the Vatican as a decent and honest man, expressed shame to Casaroli over what he considered to be Mobutu's betrayal in a public speech of his guarantee to the Vatican regarding the Cardinal's right to return. At this point, Casaroli expressed great pessimism to me about the rapid deterioration of GOZ-Church relations and for the country's future in general. He sadly feared that Mobutu, after such a hopeful beginning, had embarked on the destructive, irrational course followed by so many other African leaders.

On his April 1972 visit, Lodge met with Cardinal Villot and Archbishop Casaroli who told him that the Pope might ask the U.S. to intercede with Mobutu in an effort to improve relations with Cardinal Malula. On the basis of a briefing on the Zaire situation from the State Department, Lodge told Benelli that in the opinion of the USG any U.S. interference at this time would be inopportune and would tend to defeat its own purpose. Benelli listened without comment, a fact that I interpreted as a lack of agreement.

Out of the blue in mid-May, the Zairian Government officially announced a full pardon for Cardinal Malula. He left Rome for Brussels on June 13 and shortly thereafter did return to Zaire. Malula failed to take a dynamic role in Church affairs after his return. Events of the previous months seemed to have taken all the fight out of him. Mobutu came to Rome a year later and informed the Holy See through his ambassador that he did wish to see the Pope but required an "official invitation." As Casaroli explained to the ambassador, the Vatican never issued invitations but that the door was always open to President Mobutu. The Pope even went so far as to inform Mobutu through Ambassador Sita that he would be willing to receive the president at any hour convenient to him. There was no way that the Vatican would violate well-established protocol and issue an invitation, something moreover that Mobutu might later display as a green light from the Vatican regarding his dealings with the Church in Zaire.

Uganda

During my tenure, the Vatican did not yet have any grave bilateral problems with Uganda's Amin regime, but they did react with concern to a number of deplorable situations in Uganda. They considered, for example, the possibility of requesting a number of countries (the U.S., Zaire, and the Federal Republic of Germany) to have their ambassadors in Kampala intervene with Amin on behalf of the recently arrested Chief Justice Kiwanuka, but before moving forward on this project they sought our advice. Although they did not see anti-Catholicism as part of the move against the Catholic Kiwanuka, the Holy See did fear the possibility in the near future of the Church in Uganda being a scapegoat, as had become the case with the dramatic Israeli rescue of its aircraft at Kampala Airport. Under instructions from the Vatican, the Nuncio in Kampala had been instructed to inform Amin that in the Vatican's view Amin's decision to expel its Asian residents from Uganda had been an inhumane act, which seriously discredited Uganda internationally.

By 1972, the Ugandan Government had begun to impose restrictions on missionary activities in the country. This was done through natural attrition, the refusal to extend residence permits and the denial of visas to new missionaries. Given the fact that Amin was not explicitly expelling missionaries but resorting to legalistic measures made it difficult for the Vatican to protest directly.

Guinea

The Lodge Mission provided considerable assistance to the Vatican in cases where members of the local Catholic hierarchies were having serious difficulties with their governments or, as in the case of Guinea, were actually incarcerated. Archbishop Raymonde-MarieTchidimbo of Conakry had the usual strained relations with the dictator Sekou Touré. By late 1970, the situation had reached such a level of hostility that the President was suspected of planning to expel Tchidimbo. By the end of December, the archbishop had been arrested and charged with treason and collusion with foreign enemies of Guinea. In addition to passing messages through the U.S. embassy at Conakry to churchmen in Guinea, the State Department was frequently consulted on the best ways to proceed in the effort to obtain Tchidimbo's release. In reality, the U.S. Embassy at Conakry was the most reliable source of information on the state of play in Guinea. In late January 1971 the Pope sent a personal appeal to Touré. At this point the archbishop was sentenced to life imprisonment for his "crimes against the state." The Vatican felt that this was tantamount to a death sentence given the conditions prevailing in Guinean prisons. Touré denied the Pope's appeal for clemency for Tchidimbo, who was only released in 1979.

Benelli expressed to me his and the Pope's deepest gratitude and appreciation for American assistance in the Tchidimbo affair.

This tragic situation had provided a golden opportunity to ingratiate ourselves with our Vatican contacts and to show how much could be achieved on matters of mutual interest. It also amply demonstrated the humanitarian value of the Lodge Mission. In our own self interest, this type of assistance built up credit on which we could draw in case we ourselves needed a special favor.

MULTILATERAL DIPLOMACY

The Vatican was a member of a number of international organizations and had observer status in others. Generally, the Vatican participated in these organizations as the Holy See, but in some cases, such as the Universal Postal Union, they participated as the Vatican City State. The Vatican also attended many international meetings to discuss a wide variety of subjects. These included the Non-Proliferation Treaty, the Law of the Sea, The Council of Security and Cooperation in Europe, and the Law of War Conference. The Holy See frequently consulted with other countries' governments to see what they suggested regarding the Holy See's adherence to a given agreement. We often suggested it would be useful for the Holy See to sign such agreements as the NPT (Non-Proliferation Treaty), which they did. In most cases, their consultations were no more than that, and it did not really require any strong persuasion to convince them to sign or participate.

So why was Vatican adherence to agreements desirable? First, because having the Holy See subscribe to an international agreement like the NPT granted it moral value in the eyes of many, and second, because a Vatican signature was often useful in moving reluctant or disinterested Catholic countries to join in. Indeed, the Vatican signature proved on occasion to be helpful in obtaining an Argentine or Spanish signature. The Pope issued a private message to the United States and to the Soviets in which he expressed his great satisfaction on the occasion of the signing of the Strategic Arms Limitation Treaty (SALT) agreement in 1971.

The Vatican showed early interest in participating in the Conference on Security and Cooperation in Europe (CSCE) and noted that the nature of their participation would depend on what other participants wished of them. Their participation would not be as a European entity but as a force of world moral opinion, deeply interested in the matters under debate. They could only participate if the others agreed that they not take part in discussions or voting of a military or political nature. From the outset, the Vatican was concerned that the United States was not participating very enthusiastically. In their opinion, the ultimate success of the conference depended on the degree of importance that the U.S. attached to it. Although he could not say so in public, Casaroli admitted to me that he felt that with the current state of East-West relations in Europe, it was sadly essential that the U.S. maintain a strong military presence. Casaroli considered the unfolding of the CSCE successful in general. He believed it to be a significant step toward creating a European moral and legal system, which would reduce Soviet aggression and make the Soviets feel more constrained to conform to standard norms of international behavior. Of major interest to the Vatican was the inclusion in the final CSCE document of language guaranteeing free movement between European countries for religious purposes, both for laity and clergy. They sought and obtained our support for this language.

In September 1972, I discussed with Casaroli our efforts to stimulate interest in concrete international measures to combat terrorism, piracy, and hijacking. I noted that I was not instructed to seek Vatican support on these measures, but that we did want the Holy See to be aware of our deep concern and our efforts to seek solutions to the present unacceptable situation. Casaroli said he feared that terrorism was becoming epidemic and that regardless of countermeasures it could not be totally extirpated until it had run its course, and until the root causes were removed. While stressing that there was never an excuse for acts of terrorism, Casaroli emphasized that such acts often stem from unacceptable conditions such as in the case of the long-unsolved problems of Palestinians. He believed there was little hope that the small groups of Palestinian terrorists would cease until an acceptable solution was found to the Palestinian problem. It was clear to me that Casaroli felt that since Israel had the upper hand in the conflict they should be more disposed to practice some restraint.

The spectrum of the political reporting covered during my five years with the Lodge mission was vast and highly challenging. The Vatican was intimately involved in any country in which a Catholic Church existed, and that, naturally, included most nations, and often the most remote areas of the world. It was clear from the outset that the Vatican was an excellent contact and that they had genuinely solid sources in their information gathering networks. Though they had no systematic methods for classifying and evaluating so much raw intelligence, the Vatican functionaries were sufficiently trained to filter out the gold from the dross.

I suspect that at first our embassies around the world were a bit surprised to suddenly start receiving a rather steady flow of information from Vatican sources about their countries of assignment. After a short while, however, this flow became commonplace and we began to receive queries from them and numerous dialogues were established. This put us solidly in the net in many critical areas, especially Eastern Europe. There is no doubt that this tiny mission, which was certainly established with very limited goals, rapidly more than justified its cost.

XIV

A Long-Term Guest Departs

Jozsef Cardinal Mindszenty, Archbishop of Esztergom and Primate of Hungary, sought political asylum in the American Legation at Budapest on November 4, 1956. Arrested in 1949, following the communist takeover of Hungary, he had been sentenced to life imprisonment. Freed at the outset of the Hungarian uprising against Soviet domination, he fled to the alerted American Embassy just before the Soviet tanks rolled in to resume control of the Hungarian capital. He was to remain as the guest of the United States Government for almost fifteen years.

For years, Mindszenty had been a living symbol of Hungarian resistance to Soviet domination, to traditional values of nationalism, and to the former status of the Roman Catholic Church. His position in the political context was strengthened by the fact that the ancient Hungarian Constitution, which he believed to be still valid, gave the Archbishop of Esztergom the right and duty to act as regent of the country during periods when either the throne was vacant or when there was no legal civil regent. It will be remembered, for example, that the pre-World War II dictator, Admiral Horthy, had the legal title of regent, also in keeping with this ancient judicial provision. Since the Cardinal considered the communist regime in Hungary illegitimate, he felt that by rights the legitimate sovereignty of the country fell to him. Due to these circumstances, Mindszenty's position, in the eyes of a vast number of Hungarians, greatly exceeded his role as the head of the Church.

The United States Government had early on decided that it would allow Cardinal Mindszenty to leave or remain in our diplomatic mission as he wished. The world famous asylum-seeker caused the United States no particular problem and presented few obstacles in our bilateral relationships with the Hungarian Government. In fact, Cardinal Mindszenty's very existence was something like the emperor's clothes; neither the Hungarians nor the Americans chose to discuss him. Given the cramped nature of the American Embassy at Budapest, it was a bit inconvenient to have a guest occupy what had been the ambassador's office, but it had been decided that the Embassy would simply live with this problem without complaint.

Mindszenty's life was very simple in our legation and later embassy. The change in the status of our representation from legation to embassy in 1967 was to Mindszenty an unwarranted legitimization of the Hungarian regime, and was one of the few times that he threatened to leave our premises. Only a visit by Cardinal Franz Koenig of Vienna managed to calm him down. His life in the embassy was basically that of a simple priest, his parish being the Catholic members of the embassy family, for whom he said mass, gave first communions, and heard confessions. His major demand on the embassy staff was a thirty-minute walk each afternoon in which an embassy officer had to accompany him. This was due to the problem that half of the embassy courtyard where he walked was under Hungarian jurisdiction and thus provided a place where the Hungarian authorities could seize him should they have so wished.

As mentioned above, the Hungarian Government had chosen not to raise the question of the Cardinal with the United States. Yet, as the Cardinal approached eighty years of age, the Hungarians' concern began to grow. It was obvious that a dead Mindszenty would be a greater problem than a live one living quietly under an American roof. How would they handle the death of such a controversial national symbol, his funeral, and his burial? The headaches would be legion. Even the question of what to do should he die in the Embassy was never discussed among any of the parties and I am uncertain whether there existed a contingency plan for this eventuality in the Embassy's files.

As time went on, the Vatican also began to see advantages in getting the Cardinal out of Hungary. His departure would present considerable leverage to the Vatican in negotiating matters of interest to them with the Hungarian Government. One matter that was at a virtual standstill was the question of filling vacant Hungarian dioceses with full residential bishops rather than with the temporary and less satisfactory solution of naming apostolic administrators. Like the U.S. Government, however, the Vatican had never put any pressure on the Cardinal to depart from his refuge.

While Cardinal Mindszenty resided at the United States Embassy, the only ranking churchman to see him was Cardinal Koenig, who visited him approximately twice yearly. Mindszenty felt that, as an Austrian and a "young man," Koenig had no meaningful understanding of circumstances in Hungary and, like the Americans and the Vatican, Koenig was naive about communism and how to deal with communist governments. Koenig, as well as the Vatican, came to understand that while Mindszenty was a truly heroic figure, he was a stubborn, unrealistic, and difficult old man.

Thus the Hungarians and the Vatican could see the advantages in acting to remove Mindszenty from the U.S. Embassy. The U.S. Government had to be convinced that the time was ripe to overcome inertia on the situation. By late 1970, our Ambassador at Budapest, Alfred Puhan, had discussed with the Hungarians the advantages to them in resolving the Mindszenty affair. In spite of America's seeming lack of interest in the matter, Puhan suggested in a message to the State Department on January 13, 1971, that we give some thought to the Cardinal's future. His message received no formal answer.

From my vantage point in the Vatican, I understood the practical advantages to be gained by all sides from moving Cardinal Mindszenty out of Hungary, but had never raised the subject with anyone, nor had I ever received any instructions to discuss this delicate issue. A unique opportunity to raise the issue presented itself on April 16, 1971.

Hungarian Foreign Minister Janos Peter had called on Pope Paul that morning, shortly after which I happened to be meeting with the Vatican's Eastern European specialist, Monsignor Giovanni Cheli. Due to Peter's visit our talk naturally turned to Hungary and Cardinal Mindszenty. I had never discussed the Cardinal with anyone at the Vatican, and the only indication I had ever received that the Church's attitude might be on the verge of changing was a rumor picked up from an American Catholic journalist that the Vatican was considering asking the U.S. to put pressure on Mindszenty to leave our embassy. As I suspected, and as Cheli's remarks made amply clear, the Vatican had no intention of applying pressure. However, the Vatican was, for the first time, giving serious consideration to finding a new approach to getting the Cardinal out of Hungary. The Vatican hoped to find the right Hungarian churchman to do the job of convincing, someone who would have the power to persuade the Cardinal, without coercion, that it was in the best interest of the Church in Hungary that he depart.

Another swaying point that the Vatican hoped to make to Mindszenty was that his treasured memoirs would never be published were he to die in the American Embassy. If he died in Hungary and the Vatican came into possession of his memoirs, it would certainly take at least fifty years before the Vatican would decide to have them published. Neither the American nor the Hungarian governments would facilitate their publication. Cheli hoped that a proposal to publish his memoirs could be offered to Mindszenty as a major inducement to depart.

Immediately after this intriguing conversation, I sent a report by letter to Ambassador Lodge. Shortly after, on April 23, I wrote a highly classified letter to Ambassador Puhan in Budapest giving him all the major points of my talk with Monsignor Cheli. On April 28, Lodge wrote me to say that he had given my letter on Mindszenty limited circulation in quarters where it was appreciated.

The most urgent and difficult task for the Vatican was to locate the suitable Hungarian cleric, someone with just the right combination of skills and personal qualities. Fortunately, the right man was found in Monsignor Jozsef Zagon, a distinguished member of the Roman Curia. Zagon was serving as Secretary of the Pontifical Commission for Migration and Tourism, one of the new agencies that had been created after the Second Vatican Council to deal with problems of the modern world. The commission handled questions of immigration, pilgrimages, migrant workers, and tourists. In addition to this function, Zagon was a Canon of St. Mary Major, a position of distinction at one of the great basilicas of Rome. Zagon had begun his career as a priest in Mindszenty's former diocese and had fled Hungary with the Cardinal's help in 1949. Mindszenty was his hero.

Intense preparations for an eventual visit to Mindszenty occupied the Vatican team throughout May. By mid-month it was decided to schedule a visit to Budapest for late June. Cardinal Koenig would go first to pave the way and also to introduce Cheli and Zagon to Mindszenty, the type of indispensable protocol gesture that the old man was sure to appreciate. Cheli insisted that Mindszenty must be advised in fairly unequivocal terms that it would best serve the interests of the Church in Hungary if he left his native land. Such a message, however, must be gentle enough not to appear like an ultimatum; the Cardinal's sensitivities had to be respected.

When I reported the above to the State Department, they replied that they were very interested that the Vatican was now considering an effort to encourage Mindszenty to depart Hungary. They also expressed appreciation for my efforts and careful reporting. I was instructed to inform Cheli that the United States looked forward to consulting through Archbishop Raimondi, the Apostolic Delegate in Washington. The following week, Cheli informed me that he had discussed the progress of the Mindszenty affair with Archbishop Casaroli, the Vatican's "foreign minister," and that Casaroli had told him that he would prefer using the Lodge mission as a channel of communication in the future. I considered this quite a vote of confidence in the utility of our little mission to further relations between the United States and the Holy See.

In early June, the Department asked me to brief Casaroli and Cheli, giving them the United States' views on how Mindszenty should be approached. Based on such long years of exposure, the U.S. considered it essential that he be offered a forceful and attractive proposal. Most important would be the possibility of editing and publishing his memoirs, even if posthumously, as he was very concerned with his place in history. Additionally, we believed that the Hungarian Government was most anxious to move quickly and would be prepared to allow the Cardinal to retain all his titles, provided he had no influence on the running of the Hungarian Church, nor engaged in politics.

As agreed, Koenig went to Budapest a few days before the arrival of Cheli and Zagon. Cheli and Zagon met with Mindszenty for three agonizing days of talks starting on June 25. Following the Pope's instructions, they did not urge him to leave but attempted to present the realities of the current situation in such a light that he himself would freely see the benefits of departing. Although Mindszenty's initial reaction to his visitors was to suspect some sort of cabal between the Vatican and the Hungarian Government to get him out, he later expressed pleasure over the assurances that he could retain his titles and work on his memoirs. As the discussions ensued, Mindszenty accepted the desirability of his leaving and expressed his willingness to sign a paper to that effect. However, he did not wish to go to Rome, but preferred to reside in nearby Vienna, at the Pazmaneum, an old Hungarian seminary that was under the jurisdiction of his diocese. He also accepted that the Vatican could name an apostolic administrator to his see of Esztergom. On the question of clemency or pardon from the Hungarian Government, he would neither seek it nor accept it; only full rehabilitation would be suitable.

Yet in spite of the foregoing, on the final day of talks, the Cardinal refused to sign any agreement regarding his departure. The Cardinal told the Ambassador that he did not feel pressured by the Pope and had understood from Cheli that he was free to make his own decision regarding his future. In the Ambassador's opinion, as expressed also to Cheli, at this point only a direct papal message would move Mindszenty to action.

In the middle of his meetings with Cheli and Zagon, Mindszenty had sent a letter written in incredibly broken English to President Nixon to inform him that the Vatican sought a change in his status. After thanking the President, the United States Government, and the American people for their many kindnesses, he asked the President for guidance in his moment of agonizing decision. He also noted that his departure could destroy the sliver of hope that his presence represented for many Hungarian emigrants and "slaves." The Ambassador suggested an answer limited to expressing our satisfaction at having been able to help and our willingness to assist him should he decide to move.

The absence of a prompt reply from the President to his letter gave Mindszenty an excuse to temporize about his decision to leave. He had tentatively agreed to receive Cheli and Zagon again on or about July 14, but as that date approached he told our Ambassador that he could not give a definitive answer about his departure until he heard from the President. Mercifully, a reply from the White House dated July 15 arrived. President Nixon expressed his and the American people's satisfaction over having been able to help the Cardinal in his moment of need, a gesture for which no thanks were necessary. The President went on to say that he realized that whatever decision "you and His Holiness" take will be done in the light of the best interests of the Church and "your concern for its ministry to the people of Hungary." In closing, the President expressed his understanding of the "difficulties involved in making your decision."

In a separate letter to the Pope, written at the same time, Mindszenty expressed his wish to remain in Hungary for the rest of his life. Nonetheless, he agreed to leave if that was considered to be in the best interests of the Church.

On July 16, Cheli and Zagon wrapped up three sessions of over five hours of strenuous negotiations during which the Cardinal finally agreed to his departure. He imposed the conditions that the world must understand that his departure resolved none of the problems of the Hungarian Church, that his sister could visit him before he left, and that his papers were to be sent safely to Vienna prior to his leaving. At this point, he was given a personal letter from the Pope welcoming his decision to leave Hungary. He also signed a pro-memorial saying he hoped to leave the American Embassy before October to reside in Vienna.

Approval was now sought and obtained from the Department of State to transfer Cardinal Mindszenty's memoirs from our Embassy at Budapest to Vienna where they would be turned over to him after his arrival. With Washington's approval, Ambassador Puhan gave a written guarantee to this effect to Mindszenty on August 25. The Cardinal accepted this letter but expressed his displeasure that it had not come from the President. A few days later, Puhan reported that his guest was in a very upset state and that he feared he might even attempt to walk out of the embassy.

In mid-September, Zagon had three more days of hard talks with the Cardinal, who was now temporizing that he really should stay to finish his memoirs as many of the original sources he required were available only in Hungary. He also felt that the planned trip to Rome to participate with the Pope at the upcoming world Synod of Bishops would be too fatiguing. Eventually, Mindszenty agreed to depart on September 27. Then on their last meeting, the Cardinal told Zagon that he really could not leave on September 27 as agreed the previous day. Puhan expressed his conviction to Zagon at this point that only a plea from the Pope would move matters forward.

Eventually, the Pope made his plea for Mindszenty's presence at the Synod of Bishops, Ambassador Puhan duly delivered the memoirs to the American Embassy at Vienna in person, and the Cardinal agreed to leave on September 28. It was arranged that he would travel to Vienna with Archbishop Rossi, the Papal Nuncio to Austria, by car.

As promised, Cardinal Mindszenty left his refuge of almost 15 years on September 28. He expressed great appreciation for America's wonderful gesture toward him. After giving small gifts to the assembled embassy staff and a leather-bound volume to the Ambassador, at 8:30 a.m. he walked briskly to the waiting

Buick. When he entered the car with Archbishop Rossi and Monsignor Zagon, he realized he had not taken the place of honor and immediately slid over. Cheli followed in another car. The Hungarian Government provided escort cars both fore and aft, the rear car with a doctor. On leaving Budapest, the car approached a crossroads with arrows reading Balaton in one direction and Esztergom in the other. He remarked wistfully, "That's not meant for me." Although assurances had been given for him to stop along the way in Hungary, he chose not to. No one along his route evinced any signs of recognition. He crossed the border into Austria non-stop without ceremony. Tears were visible in his eyes as he left his country for good. Mindszenty flew from Vienna to Rome in the reserved first class compartment of an Alitalia plane with the Vatican party and Archbishop Casaroli, who had joined them in Vienna.

I joined the Vatican Secretary of State, Cardinal Villot, and other top officials in the VIP lounge of the Rome Airport to await the arrival of the flight from Vienna. Villot was wiping sweat from his brow, seemingly not too happy at the prospect of his meeting/confrontation with the arriving guest. There were about 30 pushy Italian cameramen and journalists waiting outside the airport. When the plane stopped on the runway, Cardinal Villot and Monsignor Gaspari of the Vatican "foreign office" entered the plane, where they remained for about five minutes. Villot descended first, then Mindszenty came down alone. About halfway down an Alitalia employee gave him a hand. Mindszenty smiled pleasantly, looking rather tired but well. When he noticed the crush of journalists he appeared visibly shaken. Still, he made the sign of the cross and gave his blessing to those present, saying in Latin, "A blessing on all you kind gentlemen come down to welcome me." He said not another word. After entering Villot's car, he sped off to the Vatican, which he entered un-noticed by the Arch of the Bells.

The day after his arrival in the Vatican, Mindszenty was in a huff. He wanted to return to Hungary. He was being used as a pawn between the Church and the Government of Hungary and that he did not want to con-celebrate mass with the Pope on September

30 in the Sistine Chapel. Zagon managed with great difficulty to get him cooled down. Following this flare-up he announced that he would like to call a press conference, but first he wished to discuss the advisability of doing so with some of the leading Hungarian émigrés living in Rome. Luckily, the five émigrés who came told him that they thought, as did Vatican officials, that the press conference was a poor idea, and he was convinced without any further effort. The émigrés also assured him he was correct in having left Hungary. He received the same opinion from some of the most conservative cardinals like Ottaviani and Antoniutti. Finally, he seemed happy and convinced of the wisdom of his departure. On October 2, he even drove to Albano, in the hills outside Rome, to visit the ailing Cardinal Tisserant.

On October 1, the Hungarian Government announced that they had granted an amnesty to Mindszenty. The Vatican immediately clarified that they had never requested this and that it was purely an initiative of Hungary's. The negotiations to free the Cardinal were limited narrowly to securing permission for his departure. As is known, the Vatican asserted, the Cardinal would never accept anything short of a total rehabilitation.

Thus concluded a most unusual fifteen-year adventure for the United States Government and our Embassy at Budapest. The return of the Crown of St. Stephan was not part of the negotiation, as this relic was in U.S. hands and the United States took no direct part in the negotiations regarding the Cardinal. That was strictly a bilateral affair between Hungary and the Vatican. However, shortly after Mindszenty's departure, Ambassador Lodge did ask the Pope if he would be willing to take the crown off our hands. We suggested jokingly that since one of his papal predecessors had originally given the crown to Hungarian King Istvan in the 10th century, it might be appropriate and useful to repeat the gesture. Pope Paul politely demurred, not wishing to get involved in another problem with the Magyars.

As a closing observation, Monsignor Cheli told me that he had never seen such a difficult and hard-headed man like Mindszenty in his life. He said that he felt sure the Cardinal would have difficulty getting along with any kind of government, including one run by his own Church. Mindszenty was difficult, yet nonetheless a hero who had been imprisoned by the Germans as an anti-Nazi and by his own country as an anti-communist traitor.

38 years later it is interesting to ask whether it had been wise to seek Cardinal Mindszenty's departure from Hungary. The United States had the least to gain and we assuredly would not have taken action had the Vatican not shown interest. When they did, however, that old American disease of impatience to solve problems, any problems, right now, took over. In addition we were in the age of detente and wanted to encourage the genuine trends of liberalization that were underway in Hungary. Even so, the United States Government never even thought to weigh various options with the Vatican; we just enthusiastically went along. Mindszenty's presence in our embassy was, after all, no major thorn in our relations with Hungary. At the time it was too tempting and also without real cost to us to encourage the Hungarian Government by such gestures as Mindszenty's departure and the return shortly after of the Crown of St. Stephen. For the Church the gains were genuine enough, but could they not have been achieved just as easily four years later when the Cardinal died? The gains for Hungary were the greatest. They were freed of a potentially massive problem should Mindszenty die in Hungary. His death might have triggered a wave of protests throughout the country and ended up pressuring the government to concede significant reforms. It is doubtful if protests would have lead to anything like the Solidarity movement in Poland 17 years later—but who knows!

In his book *The Cardinal in the Chancery and Other Stories*, Ambassador Puhan gave rather detailed and accurate coverage to the above events. He was not, however, in a position to describe the action in the Vatican nor the question of how the process got started through the Lodge mission. The above, to the best of my knowledge, covers these matters fully for the first time. Cardinal Mindszenty's published memoirs, very disappointing and "unexplosive" as a matter of fact, leave out many important details.

Secretary of State William Rogers call on the Pope

XV

The Middle East and Jerusalem

No area of this troubled world was of more natural interest to the Holy See than the Holy Land, sacred to Christians and essential for the practice of Christianity in the context of pilgrimages and the proper maintenance of the holy sites. The Catholic Church continues to be a key player in the Holy Land and takes part in managing many of the main religious sites connected with the life of Jesus and the early Church. A top official of the Church is the Latin Patriarch of Jerusalem, who is named by the Vatican and who has overall responsibility for overseeing the many holy sites and religious institutions under his watchful care.

The Vatican followed very closely all the vicissitudes of the struggle for a just solution to the Israeli-Palestinian problem, but they did not advocate any specific solutions beyond their often-expressed wish that the holy sites in and around Jerusalem be government by some sort of international statute. It must be recalled that all the way back in 1948, the United Nations also supported this. So just what did the Vatican mean by internationalization? They were never completely specific, but suggested that all of the old city of Jerusalem plus the major religious sites nearby be governed under some sort of special statute or regime and not simply by Israel. The Vatican also felt that an international body should provide a court of appeals for disputes arising regarding the governance of the holy sites. In their eyes, such a body could be the World Court at The Hague or even the United Nations. They believed that Jerusalem should be a center of monotheists, a place where Christians, Jews, and Muslims could live and mingle happily in a fully ecumenical environment. An equally important consideration was that Christians should continue to inhabit Jerusalem and other traditional Christian communities in the Holy Land. The Vatican was very worried about the "Zionization" of Jerusalem, and did not wish to have a situation created in which Christian pilgrims would visit a place where virtually everyone they came into contact with was an Israeli Jew. Under no circumstances would the Vatican be satisfied with a solution that merely gave each faith the control of their own religious sites.

Shortly after my arrival, on July 15, 1970, I learned from Monsignor Joseph Gremillion that he would be visiting Jerusalem officially to explore the possibilities for discussing with the Israeli Government the internationalization of Jerusalem. His contact there was the Apostolic Delegate, Archbishop Pio Laghi. Gremillion told me that he realized the internationalization of Jerusalem was secondary to the problems of withdrawal from Palestinian territory and the return of Palestinian refugees, but he believed that if progress on Jerusalem could be achieved between Israel and the Palestinians, this might have a salutary effect in moving the same parties forward on other questions. He mentioned the desirability of a joint declaration on Jerusalem by the religious leaders of the three major faiths, but recognized the difficulty of finding a Muslim spokesman with sufficient weight. Personally, I thought it would be equally difficult to find a Jewish religious leader to sign on to any such declaration. When he asked me what the United States' position on internationalization was, I replied that while we were not pushing for it, we did believe that Old Jerusalem should remain undivided, with special roles for a future Palestinian state, Israel, and Jordan. Ideally, after determining Jerusalem's boundaries, these countries should work out some joint arrangement for administering the city. The United States further believed that free movement for Israelis and Palestinians should be guaranteed as well as free access to all religious shrines for the members of all faiths. Gremillion said that he found the United States' position reasonable and would use it as a basis for his own efforts.

During a March 1971 audience, the Pope told Lodge that he was very distressed over what he termed the "Zionization" of Jerusalem. He felt it was very important that non-Jews remain a strong presence in the city. He wanted to protect these people, whom he felt were actually being boycotted by the Israelis, and he believed that internationalization was the answer. His definition of internationalization was virtually identical to Gremillion's. The Pope said that other leaders were pressing the Church to take the lead on the future of Jerusalem, but he did not want to create friction. One idea that he had rejected was to flood Jerusalem with organized pilgrimages; something he also felt would be a fruitless irritant to the Israelis.

Other Vatican officials agreed with the Pope's insistence that a vibrant Christian community must remain in Jerusalem, especially since many of these Christians were descendents of the Jews who first converted to Christianity in the 1st century. The Vatican was convinced that Israel was consciously and cynically attempting to crush the Arab Christian community in Jerusalem. It was difficult for foreign missionary teachers to obtain Israeli permission to teach at Christian Arab schools. Additionally, Israel recognized Jewish religious holidays, but gave no consideration to Christians from police or local authorities for their processions or other public manifestations.

Occasional papal statements on the future of Jerusalem adhered closely to the above policies. During my five-year tenure, I had occasion to report these views to our missions in Israel and to the White House. Even after leaving Rome, I prepared a policy suggestion, for the internationalization of Jerusalem, which I knew would be acceptable to the Holy See. I even included suggestions for a seal and flag for the internationalized Jerusalem. I also shared this plan with my old friend, Zbigniew Brzezinski, who was then head of the National Security Council. He thanked me, noting that the White House had a substantial file of Jerusalem proposals.

When Israeli Prime Minister Golda Meir saw the Pope in January 15, 1973, they had a cordial meeting but differed sharply on the future of Jerusalem and Palestinian refugees. Vatican fears that the Israelis would attempt to exploit the audience for their own purposes led the Vatican to issue a strong press statement immediately following the meeting. Although the language, even by Vatican admission, was unnecessarily sharp, the Israelis did not seem displeased. The statement was geared, and successfully so, to get the Vatican off the hook with their Arab friends. On arrival in Tel Aviv, Mrs. Meir reacted to the Vatican press release by letting her hair down in an interview with the Israeli weekly *Ma'ariv*. Yet after everyone had let off steam, both the Vatican and Mrs. Meir seemed to agree the audience with the Pope was a positive step in Catholic-Jewish relations, even though the Vatican did not change its insistence on some type of internationally recognized statute for Jerusalem.

In a press conference following the audience, Mrs. Meir denied that she had sought the papal audience, a point that the Vatican firmly rejected. The Vatican stated publicly that "the Pope accepted Mrs. Meir's request because he believed that it is his duty not to lose any opportunity to work on behalf of peace and in defense of the rights of the human person, and of communities, to defend the religious interests of all and especially to help the weakest and most defenseless—in first place the Palestinian refuges. Regarding the defense and custody of religious interests, it should not be necessary to recall that in this specific case one is dealing with the native and inalienable rights of three monotheistic religions connected with the universal and pluralistic character proper for Jerusalem." During his meeting with Mrs. Meir, the Pope did not fail to note the long history of suffering of the Jewish people.

In the final analysis, the Vatican considered the main accomplishment of the meeting the mere fact that it took place at all. One of the grounds for issuing a strong press statement was to scotch the fear that the Israelis would twist the audience in such a way as to imply some changes in the Vatican's position on such issues as Jerusalem. Additionally, in her press conference Mrs.

Meir denied the Vatican contention that she had taken advantage of her visit to Paris to add on a stop in Rome.

After a week of letting the dust settle, I began to work on an assessment of the Meir visit. One highly-informed European ambassador told me that it was a "masterpiece of exactly how not to handle a high level visit to the Vatican." Casaroli told another contact of mine that it was a cordial meeting, and "using the communist meaning of the phrase, a frank exchange of ideas," with neither side modifying its position. The story of who invited whom ended up appearing a bit cagey. The most I got out of Casaroli was that "these things just developed naturally during a series of conversations." I suspect that both sides were happy to have the meeting, certainly neither wanted to be placed in the position of having to refuse it, and all were willing to deal afterwards with any discomfort caused by comments about the meeting from the opposite side.

Casaroli told me that as he escorted Mrs. Meir from her car through the long rows of exquisite Vatican apartments to the Pope's office, he had the chance to converse amiably with her. At one point, she commented to Casaroli that she was probably the first Jewish woman to be honored there. Casaroli replied that, no, that was not really quite accurate, for the most honored woman in the Vatican was the Virgin Mary, without question a Jewish lady of some renown. Mrs. Meir laughed and made no further comment.

Rumors started circulating in November 1973 that President Nimeiri of Sudan and Emperor Haile Selassie of Ethiopia would be calling on the Pope to stress the need for some sort of special status for Jerusalem. Finally, on December 17 the two leaders plus President Kaunda of Zambia requested an audience, which was immediately granted. The audience was set for December 22, and only one day before, Vice-President Greene of Liberia also joined the group. The visit was to be very low-key without any media attention. The purpose of the visit was to discuss the Middle East, with special emphasis on Jerusalem as well as racism and colonization in Africa. The hope was that the Vatican would attend the Geneva negotiations on the Middle East and make known publicly their strong support for an ecumenical Jerusalem. The audience ended up lasting a significant 90 minutes. In addition to the discussions on Jerusalem, the visitors also asked the Pope to counsel moderation to the Portuguese on Africa. Casaroli told me that it was the first time that the Pope had received more than one principal guest and had sat down around a table for an informal discussion. Casaroli continued that the African leaders had praised the Pope for his deep interest in Africa's welfare and for his statements counseling moderation and peace in Mozambique. They also expressed pleasure at the Pope's appeal for self-determination and independence in his December 21 speech to the cardinals. In conclusion, the guests expressed the hope that the Pontiff would continue his interest in Africa and also asked that he use his influence with the Catholic Portuguese to counsel a more reasonable approach toward their African territories.

At the conclusion of the above discussion, Casaroli recalled to me that in his conversation with Portuguese Foreign Minister Patricio at the Non-Proliferation Treaty (NPT) talks in Helsinki, he was astonished at the apparent depth of Portuguese conviction over the rectitude of what they were doing in Africa. This made discussions with the Portuguese difficult. Yet, the factor that gave the Holy See the greatest concern in Portuguese Africa was the fate of the large number of black Africans who were cooperating with Portugal. These Africans frequently expressed to the Church their fears of being liquidated should there be independence.

Excellent Jewish Contacts

I had two particularly good contacts from the Jewish side: Dr. Joseph Lichten and Mr. Meir Mendes of the Israeli Embassy to Italy. Dr. Lichten had been a pre-war Polish diplomat and was in Rome as the representative of the Anti-Defamation League of B'nai B'rith. Mendes was an Israeli diplomat in his embassy in Rome, where he had the special task of following Vatican affairs. This was very appropriate for him since his father had been a friend and classmate of Pius XII when they were boys. When the Mussolini Government began to pass laws against Italian Jews the Pope had arranged with the British for Mendes senior to immigrate to Palestine. I became close friends with these two fine men and we saw a great deal of each other both socially and professionally.

First Contacts with Islamic Leaders

The ice was broken between Saudi religious leaders and the Vatican in April 1974 when Cardinal Sergio Pignedoli, President of the Vatican's Secretariat for Non-Christians, made contacts with the Saudi Ulema, or Council of Religious Scholars, and also had a warm meeting with King Feisal in Riyadh. In September of that year, he visited Cairo and met with the Supreme Council for Islamic Affairs. In late October, a delegation of the Saudi Ulema visited the Vatican for five days, during which they met with a wide range of top officials to discuss not only religious matters but also questions of human rights. The visit terminated with a very cordial audience with the Pope, who praised the efforts of his guests to raise awareness of human rights violations and ended by sending his warm greetings to the King of Saudi Arabia. Quite surprisingly, according to our sources, the questions of Jerusalem or the holy places were not discussed. The above meetings with Saudi leaders were of great interest to the Vatican, as it was perceived that tension was growing in places like Africa where Catholic and Islamic waves of conversion were coming into contact.

Another unusual ecumenical gathering was a meeting in Rome at the end of August 1972 for Christians, Muslims, and Jews. Mayor Teddy Kollek of Jerusalem attended this highly secret gathering that the Anglican Archbishop of Jerusalem Appleton had organized. Archbishop Benelli, who expressed to me his pleasure that the meeting had remained totally secret, said it was the first time that leaders of the three great monotheistic faiths had sat down together to discuss the problems of the Holy Land. Kollek met with a number of high-level Vatican officials but did not have an audience with the Pope.

During this period, the Vatican made a serious effort to develop ties with Muslim religious leaders from a variety of countries, including, as noted above, Saudi Arabia. The Pope, on a few occasions, also received a representative of the PLO, but on at least one occasion did so in the most painless manner by receiving a Palestinian Christian who had been in Rome to attend the 1974 World Food Conference. From time to time the Vatican warned me about their fears that there would be another war between Israel and their Arab neighbors, a war that the Israelis would start. One contact told me that if the United States supported Israel in any such ill-advised venture, the Arab oil-producing states were sure to institute a petroleum blockade against us.

To give balance to their relations with the Arab world, in October 1974, the Vatican created a Commission for Religious Relations with Judaism. This new organization was given a boost when Rabbi Abraham M. Hershberg, Chairman of the International Interfaith Committee on Peace and Religion, visited Rome in January 1975. Hershberg, an obvious liberal and progressive in matters of interfaith dialogue, deeply impressed his Vatican hosts with his impressive number of Muslim contacts. Vatican officials saw in Hershberg a potential bridge between Christians, Muslims, and Jews. In general, our Jewish contacts were pleased with the establishment of the commission but noted that it had a number of shortcomings in Jewish eyes, such as a failure to mention the State of Israel and its importance to Jews in a religious sense.

In 1973, I had an interesting and wide-ranging conversation with the *Chargé d'Affaires* of the Egyptian Embassy to the Holy See that seemed very prophetic for what we are trying to deal with in the Middle East today. He gave a long description of Arab grievances against Israel and what he considered America's excessive and unquestioning support for Israeli positions. In his view, it was one thing for the U.S. to supply Israel materially in order to maintain a defensive balance with the Arabs, but it was another thing when the U.S. went to the extreme of giving them sophisticated weapons, which could only be considered offensive. He felt that if the U.S. simply exerted some pressure on the Israelis, they would quickly come to a reasonable agreement with their Arab neighbors. I told my contact that the U.S. certainly was doing nothing to encourage Israeli aggressiveness, only providing weapons that we thought necessary to maintain a balance with Israel's potential adversaries.

His reply was that the facts were not always important; it was what the Arab people believed. Regrettably, throughout the Arab world, those who were previously favorably disposed toward the United States were beginning to turn against America because of our policy of supporting unquestionably their enemies in Israel. He said that Arab countries certainly had no desire to become satellites of any country, least of all of the Soviet Union. This had been amply demonstrated in 1972 when President Sadat had asked the Soviet advisers to leave the country, not as a result of any outside pressure, but in response to his own judgment.

My Egyptian contact criticized our abstention on the Security Council resolution condemning terrorism. He then went on to assert that the latest Israeli raids on Beirut were worse than the so-called terrorism organized by a liberation movement like the PLO. Most Arabs, he said, were convinced that the U.S. had a meaningful part in preparing the Israeli raid, and that, at the least, American intelligence certainly knew in advance and should have warned the Lebanese Government. I told him this was all part of a big lie technique, as evidenced by a speech that Colonel Gadaffi had recently made. The last thing the United States wanted to do was to weaken the internal stability of Lebanon, a government with which we had long-standing friendly ties, I concluded. Nevertheless, he replied, the U.S. had not been able to give credible evidence to show that we were not involved in the Israeli raids.

The conversation continued with the warning that both the United States and Israel were taking too lightly President Sadat's preparations for a new military offensive to recover occupied Egyptian territories. It was impossible for Egypt to tolerate any longer a situation of neither war nor peace, and although the struggle would be long and difficult, he assured me that those who doubted Sadat's seriousness would be sadly surprised in the near future. The situation had changed greatly since 1967; Egypt now possessed the military power to inflict serious damage to all major Israeli cities. His predictions for the future closed with the statement that the undiminished crude oil supply could not be guaranteed should there be no forward movement in settling the Arab-Israeli dispute. It's dramatic to note that a within a few months, the entire scenario he predicted became a reality!

Regarding the overall situation in the Middle East, as it pertained to the United States, my Egyptian contact noted that America's welcome in the area could not last forever. If relations with Israel were not normalized, the situation would become intolerable for traditional conservative monarchist governments, and more intractable violently nationalist ones, not friendly to the United States, would replace them. There is no doubt whatsoever, he claimed, that Arab governments recognized Israel's right to exist and would even sit down to negotiate if Israel had not in advance set down preconditions that were unacceptable. Thus, vital issues like Jerusalem, Golan Heights, and Sharm-al-Shaykh were off the table, making it impossible to initiate talks.

XVI

American Prisoners of War

Without a doubt, the main bilateral interest of the Lodge Mission revolved around the drawn-out conflict in South-East Asia. Within that context, efforts on behalf of American prisoners-of-war in Vietnam took front rank. During his first visit to Rome in July 1970, Ambassador Lodge made serious efforts to urge the Pope and other Vatican officials he met to do all within their power to alleviate the plight of our prisoners, to facilitate the movement of mail and packages, and, in the long-run, to arrange for their liberation. During my entire five years in Rome, I received frequent visits from prisoner advocates and members of prisoners' families.

One of the earliest visits, on October 13, 1970, was by Mrs. E.E. Cappelli, the wife of a prisoner of war. She had elicited the help of the Italian Red Cross, which conceived the novel idea of acting for the families of Italian-American prisoners. Their two-pronged approach consisted of sending two letters regarding each prisoner, one from the family in the U.S. and the other from alleged relatives in Italy. While I never heard anything further on this novel type of approach, it was clearly not very appropriate to have used the names of bogus Italian relatives.

When Senator Percy visited with ranking Vatican officials in mid-November 1970, he also raised the issue of our prisoners of war. Both Cardinal Secretary of State Villot and Archbishop

Casaroli told Percy that all efforts by Vatican representatives to discuss the POW issue with the North Vietnamese delegation in Paris had been rebuffed on the grounds that "all the prisoners are war criminals." Casaroli further noted that when the Pope had tried to discuss Vietnam recently with Gromyko, the latter had merely parroted North Vietnamese demands for total and immediate U.S. withdrawal. Gromyko also claimed that our men were not prisoners of war but rather war criminals and thus not covered by the Geneva Conventions. Casaroli noted that he detected an element of impotency in what the Soviets seemed to feel they could do to influence Hanoi.

At this same time, Ambassador Lodge had called his old friend the Italian Ambassador to Greece, d'Orlandi, to ask after his health following a recent heart attack. D'Orlandi took the occasion to report that he had recently received "feelers" from the North Vietnamese and asked whether Lodge might be able to come to Athens to discuss this matter which could not be dealt with on the telephone. Lodge reported this to Kissinger by letter of November 19, with the observation that d'Orlandi was an entirely solid diplomat, and that Lodge believed it was a mistake for the Kennedy Administration not to have used this channel in early 1968. Nothing came of the matter as Washington decided not to explore it.

At a lunch at the Belgian Embassy to the Holy See, Lodge met the Belgian Ambassador to the Food and Agriculture Organization (FAO), Rene van Hauwermeiren, who spoke at length about Mr. Aubrac, the Inspector General of the FAO, who had been a close friend of Ho Chi Minh and who had reportedly instigated the Paris talks. Hauwermeiren noted that Aubrac was still in good standing with the North Vietnamese and offered to arrange a meeting for Lodge. Lodge, however, was non-committal. Coincidentally, a few days earlier, Cardinal Villot had also informed Lodge, as well as Senator Percy, of Aubrac's presence in Rome. Lodge duly reported the foregoing to Kissinger, who sent his thanks and expressed the hope that the forthcoming and flexible attitude Aubrac detected and that he seemingly passed on to the Vatican would be reflected in the ongoing talks in Paris, where the North Vietnamese had every opportunity to discuss the matter with us should they so wish.

A few days later, van Hauwermeiren sent a hand-written note to Lodge at the Grand Hotel stating that he had met with Aubrac, who stressed the good relations he continued to have with the top leadership of the NVN, the unstated implication being that he could be a valid interlocutor. We did not take up Aubrac's offer. At the time, I felt that it was worthwhile to pursue any channel open to us in an effort to move forward the critical question of communicating with our prisoners. Nonetheless, one could just as easily have accepted Washington's position that the North Vietnamese could speak to us in Paris if they were so disposed.

At Lodge's request, the Pope agreed to pass a message on behalf of our POWs to the North Vietnamese Delegation in Paris on January 1, 1971, the World Day of Peace. The Pope had also originally considered including a plea for our prisoners in his traditional New Year's message, but decided that to do so would be imprudent. As was frequently the case, the DRV failed to answer the Pope's message.

A delightful Italian official of Caritas International, the Catholic Church's welfare and air organization, headquarters in Rome, whom we worked with off and on over the years, was Dr. Angiolo Salvidio. He first called on me of his own initiative following a trip to Pakistan. Purely from good will, he had decided to dedicate his attention to our prisons while in Pakistan and had raised the matter with both Vatican and Pakistani officials during his trip there. He also discussed what Caritas might do with its President, Monsignor Jean Rodhain, and with the Director General, Monsignor Maurice Bonneric. Thereafter, Caritas informed the Vatican Secretariat of State that they stood ready to be useful in any way the Secretariat may think suitable. A former civilian employee of NATO, Salvidio also seemed well-connected with a number of American ambassadors. In fact, it was our then-ambassador at Bangkok, Leonard Ungar, who had suggested he look me up. Salvidio had clearly discussed ways to help with numerous Vatican and Caritas officials and noted that all were openly willing to try to be helpful. He, personally, felt that as an action organization, Caritas was best suited to play a constructive role and could work with the Indian Red Cross. In the end, India demurred as they were overwhelmed with Pakistani refugees. General Maitra of the Indian Red Cross told Salvidio, "You ask me to help a handful of American prisoners when millions of sick and starving Pakistanis are inundating us."

The flood in North Vietnam in the fall of 1971 gave Salvidio hope that Caritas could do something by tying aid for the flood victims to some gesture for our prisoners, such as sending gifts and packages to them. The Vatican desk officer for Vietnam presented a request for the Pope to send packages in his name to our prisoners, but cautioned that only the most discreet efforts would likely be acceptable to Hanoi. He felt that many of our efforts had failed because they were aimed at shaming the North Vietnamese into acting correctly. German Caritas was, however, totally pessimistic about getting packages to our men for Christmas 1971. Monsignor Rodhain of *Caritas Internationalis* requested a visa to visit North Vietnam and promised to try to speak with our prisoners if the visa were granted.

Salvidio moved doggedly ahead. He requested a visa to visit Hanoi first in Delhi and later followed up in Laos. In the latter capital he spoke at length with a Mr. Giap and ended up informing Giap that he also hoped to see American POWs. Giap then politely repeated the usual Hanoi line about American aggression, prisoners as war criminals, etc. He also stressed that our prisoners were receiving the best attention possible under wartime conditions in North Vietnam. Salvidio replied that it would be useful even to the Democratic Republic of Vietnam (DRV) to have a neutral observer see the prisoners and publicly verify the situation. Salvidio stressed that he represented the Holy See and Caritas, that his purpose in wishing to see the prisoners was purely humanitarian, and that even were they criminals, which he personally did not believe, this would have no bearing since the Catholic Church was as concerned with the welfare of criminals as it was with prisoners of war. Salvidio was forced to return to Rome before obtaining an answer to his visa request.

When Lodge saw the Pope on April 7, 1972, he asked the Pope to seek to send a Catholic priest to DRV to minister to our prisoners. Since the United States was convinced that papal interventions had been instrumental in improving the flow of mail to our prisoners, Lodge hoped that the Vatican could now seek DRV agreement to having books and games also sent. The Pope promised to do everything in his power to help our men.

The Vatican did not begin planning for trying to send packages to our men for Christmas until mid-November. The reason for the late start was the elections in the United States; the Vatican was apparently fearful that President Nixon might be temped to use in his campaign the fact that he was working successfully with the Vatican on behalf of our prisoners. This cautious approach, of course, led to great delays; by December 12 nothing had yet been done! We also asked Archbishop Benelli if Caritas could try to deliver parcels to our prisoners in South Vietnam, Laos, and North Vietnam.

There were occasional signs that the DRV did not object to the Vatican involving itself in the Vietnamese conflict as long as its interventions were balanced and limited to peace and humanitarian concerns and not political ones. For example, when the Preus group (Dr. J.A.O. Preus was President of the Lutheran Church - Missouri Synod) called on the Pope, a meeting that had been discussed previously with the DRV *Chargé* in Stockholm, it was decided that the Vatican would give no public mention of the audience unless the DRV *Chargé* agreed. This he readily did, and the audience was published in the *Osservatore Romano*. The DRV *Chargé* in Stockholm seemed to have been at least slightly impressed by the fact that Preus represented "over 100 million U.S. Christians."

An amusing sidelight of the prisoner effort was the interest stirred between the two ancient religious orders founded originally for the purpose of ransoming prisoners being held captive by Muslims. The Trinitarians and the Mercedarians were both founded around 1200, but in modern times had becoming essentially dedicated to education. At the 775th anniversary of the Trinitarians in Rome, it was decided that the question of prisoners of conscience had grown to such proportions that the order should give serious consideration to returning to its original work on behalf of prisoner release. It was decided that initially special interest should be accorded to the plight of clergymen being held in Eastern Europe, Brazil, and China. However, they never really got this project off to a start.

To summarize, there is no question that the Vatican made herculean efforts to alleviate the plight of our prisoners of war in DRV captivity, but the results were far short of the goals. The most significant progress was made in increasing the flow of mail to and from our prisoners. In typical fashion, the North Vietnamese tried to gain as much as they could from their contacts with various Catholic emissaries and give in exchange as little as possible. Nonetheless, the DRV obviously did see something to be gained, at a minimum in public image, from being seen to cooperate in a humanitarian effort. I, therefore, have no doubt that the situation of our prisoners would have been at least marginally worse without the efforts made by the Holy See, Caritas, and other Catholic organizations.

Not quite a prisoner of war, Lawrence K. Lunt, an American citizen who had been sentenced to 30 years imprisonment in 1966 for counter-revolutionary activity in Cuba, gave considerable concern to our mission. Lunt's wife was from a well-connected Belgium family, so there was more than just American interest involved. From time to time, we sought Vatican interventions with the Cubans to obtain Lunt's release. We also explored the possibility of arranging his release in exchange for the release of Pedro Rodríguez Peralta, a Cuban captain captured in Guinea-Bissau in 1969 and in a Portuguese prison at the time. The Papal representative in Havana, Bishop Cesare Zacchi, had various conversations with the Cubans, including some with President Dorticós, yet nothing ensued. Dorticós even denied at one point that Cuba would ever release such an implacable enemy as Lunt, even in exchange for Peralta. Despite this statement from the president, the Vatican felt that if we could convince the Portuguese to release Peralta, the Cubans would reciprocate by releasing Lunt.

Our mission first became involved in the Lunt case in early 1974, just months before the overthrow of the Portuguese dictatorship. In Lisbon, our embassy tried unsuccessfully to obtain a definitive answer from the Portuguese regarding their intentions concerning Peralta. In spite of a great deal of high-level effort on his behalf and considerable imagination on ways that might be tried to secure his release, Mr. Lunt was only freed from his Cuban prison in 1979.

Robert Illing and the Pope with a White House staff member

XVII

The Population Conundrum

Unquestionably, one of the most sensitive issues we followed at the Vatican was population growth, or to be more specific, the subject of artificial birth control and the Church's official opposition to any relaxation of its blanket prohibitions. The modern debate goes back to the discussions that preceded Pope Paul's issuance of his controversial encyclical letter *Humanae Vitae* in July 1968. Preceding the publication of the encyclical, a body of some 80 renowned theologians from all over the world conducted lengthy studies. Reportedly, the vast majority of these theologians agreed that there were no concrete doctrinal grounds for a total opposition to birth control on the part of the Church so long as a married couple did not follow a policy of having no children at all. The Pope, who had to make the final decision, however, opted to side with the tiny minority of theologians who favored traditional Church teaching on the subject, and he left existing policies unchanged. To date we have no resolution to this problem, but it is obvious that the vast majority of Catholic couples in the developed world have opted not to follow the official line.

Through Cardinal Secretary of State Jean Villot, the Vatican issued unequivocal instructions to Church leaders worldwide that the official policies against all means of artificial birth control were to be scrupulously respected. In reality, the Vatican had much reason to believe that they were not alone in their intransigence.

Only the Dutch, Belgians, Germans, Canadians, and some French had expressed strong disagreement to the Vatican over the official birth control policy. Church leaders in the United States had generally not expressed themselves strongly either way. On the other hand, a high percentage of churchmen from the third world had strongly applauded Pope Paul's firm stand. Based on a purely political approach and the number of supporters in the worldwide Church the Pope's position did not seem entirely irrational. Unfortunately, as we knew, this was a lopsided approach to the problem.

In general, liberal Catholics recognized that Pope Paul had painted himself into a corner on birth control, and therefore realized that it was unrealistic to expect him to make any dramatic changes in his views. One of the two lady members of the Justice and Peace Commission tried to appeal to Pope Paul on the birth control question. He turned a saddened face to her and said, "Even you, my dear, have abandoned me." Thus all hope was pinned on his eventual successor. In spite of this discouraging situation, liberals hoped that the Pope would not exacerbate the birth control polemic during the remainder of his pontificate. They were not reassured by events!

As an aside, Monsignor Gremillion told me that the Vatican received many letters over the years from private Catholic groups in the United States complaining about the laxity of American bishops in attacking birth control and abortion legislation in the United States. These American Catholics thought the Catholic hierarchy in America should begin actively lobbying against legislation and practices that conflicted with official Catholic teachings.

Within the walls of the Vatican and in many national churches, the debate continued to rage. There formed a discreet but nevertheless somewhat revolutionary lobby within the Vatican that advocated change. An English priest, Father Arthur McCormack, was one of the leaders of this hardy band of revolutionaries. As discreet as he was, he sometimes locked horns rather frontally with the other side within the Vatican. His most virulent nemesis was a Swiss Dominican named Henri de Riedmatten and what they not only thought but said about each other had no place in a respectable Church newspaper. The battles raged sharply within the Vatican for years with no notable progress visible. Our efforts, limited to trying to remain informed and to providing information to our Vatican contacts, did little to change the Vatican's stubborn position.

Father McCormack was a strong advocate of the urgent need for effective birth control, and he had been actively lobbying behind the scenes for an overhaul of the Church's obdurate opposition. His books and articles presented a liberal Catholic viewpoint on the subject. Over the years, McCormack had learned to act with caution and, at times, secrecy; nevertheless, he had on occasion run into sharp opposition and even hostility from some members of the clergy. Although he was not certain of Archbishop Benelli's intimate feelings concerning birth control, McCormack had always enjoyed Benelli's support and felt that were Benelli in a position to determine policy in this matter his stand would have tended more toward the liberal side. Father McCormack told me that at one time he had received strong criticism from the only American Cardinal in the Curia, John Wright, but that he subsequently established a better relationship with him. Wright was known to be quite cool on the birth control issue, perhaps because African-Americans, with whom he had often worked, frequently opposed birth control on the grounds that it was merely a plot by racists to limit the size of black families.

At the time, according to McCormack, there was a considerable amount of theological gymnastics going on. Cardinal O'Boyle of Washington and a group of 19 dissident priests provided an excellent example of this. McCormack had seized upon a theological concept, subsequently elaborated by Cardinal Wright, that would allow circumventing the Church's opposition to artificial birth control. Cardinal Wright's resolution of the issue of the 19 stated, "Particular circumstances surrounding an objectively evil human act, while they cannot make it objectively virtuous, can make it inculpable, diminished in guilt or subjectively defensible." Father McCormack felt that this could permit one to say, yes, the Church is opposed to birth control as morally wrong, but in certain circumstances, the situation is such that one cannot be blamed for violating it. He gave as an example the case of a woman in the slums of Lima, a devoted Catholic who wishes to observe the teaching of *Humanae Vitae* but at the same time knows that she should practice responsible parenthood (but has not the means to do so according to Catholic teaching). This woman may, without guilt, use other methods not sanctioned by the Church. He did not see this as a long-range answer to the problem but felt that it might provide some immediate relief. McCormack thought that the Church should have concentrated attention on abortion and permitted birth control. Yet he feared that the subject had become so highly charged within the Vatican that no one wanted to discuss it. Some fatalistic theologians simply felt that as bad as overpopulation was, it was the will of God. McCormack proved sadly mistaken in his belief that Cardinal Wright's theological gymnastics could be used to justify birth control; the Cardinal, after observing the use being made of his ruling, quickly denied it had any relevance to the dispute on artificial birth control.

Pope Paul, in McCormack's opinion, was thoroughly and inalterably opposed to artificial birth control. This was a principled moral stand, which permitted no discussion. Yet many within the Vatican continued to try to broach the matter. During a meeting with the Pope, Cardinal Suenens tried as he had on other occasions to raise the issue, but the Pope refused outright to discuss it. Johannes Schauff, a wealthy German on the Justice and Peace Commission, told some colleagues on the Commission that he would like to make a plea to the Pope on birth control. He felt that he had some likelihood of success since he would be speaking as a father of six with numerous grandchildren. His colleagues dissuaded him after demonstrating that such an appeal would be completely futile. In McCormack's eyes, *Humanae Vitae* was a disastrous document, yet he had always refrained from publicly attacking it, feeling that he could accomplish more by working within the system. Ultimately, McCormack was deeply saddened because he saw his birth control stand poisoning the world against a Pope who was in general a truly a great man.

The lengthy preparations for the World Population Conference in Bucharest in August 1974 were the focal point of much of our work at the Lodge mission. We advised and hosted a number of groups and individuals who came from the United States, trying to assure that the Vatican would attend and insisting that the Vatican could play a constructive role. Philander Claxton, the State Department's point man on population matters, was our main Washington contact, and we helped him to work closely with Father McCormack. In general, we were all on the same wavelength.

Many progressives with whom we spoke considered the Church's stand on birth control as the major divisive issue in the Church, even going so far as to label it another Galileo case, capable of shaking the Church to its foundations and doing irreparable damage. This issue not only divided the Church internally, they believed, but pitted it against the forces of logic and reason in the modern world. Admittedly, many bishops ignored official opposition and permitted their priests to look the other way on transgressions. This, however, was no real solution and frequently bred contempt for the Church.

It is important to remember that clergy could be progressive on theological issues, on social issues, or on both. For instance, the Pope was unquestionably progressive on social issues, but moderately conservative theologically. The question often hinged on whether a churchman considered birth control a social or a theological issue. Although keenly aware of the negative consequences of the Church's position on birth control, the Pope felt obliged to support a generally conservative line. Yet, until the Church reversed its stand on population control, according to the progressives, it would be barred from assuming an unqualified leading position as a world moral force. Progressives considered the Pope very unwise for issuing *Humanae Vitae* on his own initiative. They would have preferred that the whole Synod of Bishops together with the Pope had considered such a weighty issue.

The progressives also feared that the leadership in the Secretariat of State was unfavorable to changes in birth control policy. They accused typical Curia officials of narrowness in understanding of world realities, which, despite their good will, kept them from realizing the gravity of their intransigence both to the Church and to international welfare. While Archbishops Benelli and Casaroli, for example, did recognize overpopulation as a serious problem, they were nonetheless unwilling to support remedies, which to them were patently immoral. Reportedly, one bishop very close to the Pope tried on twelve different occasions to impress upon the Holy Father the serious nature of the problem and the errors of the Church's official policy. The atmosphere between them became so strained that they were obliged to drop the subject from their conversations. In spite of the Pope's unquestioned and agonizing concern for the problem of development and human suffering, he was allegedly unable to find any justification for a relaxation of his moral stand against artificial means of birth control.

Some Vatican sources saw another threat to implementing birth control: the widespread belief equating strength with a large population, regardless of how miserable that population may be. They saw this idea as entrenched throughout the underdeveloped world, especially in Latin America. Many Latin Americans had observed to officials of the Pontifical Commission for Justice and Peace that only when their countries had populations of 100-200 million would the United States and other world powers take sufficient notice of them. They pointed to China as an example of this theory. Logical arguments indicating that China was feared not because of its numbers, but because of its military power fell on deaf ears. Exponents of this viewpoint also viewed birth control as a form of imperialism from the larger developed countries. A few of our contacts worried that this attitude could become a greater obstacle to birth control than were religious proscriptions and would survive even if the latter were abolished. Even such an outspoken progressive as Archbishop Helder Câmara of Brazil was so nationalistic that he favored unlimited growth of Brazil's population as a means of making it a power to be reckoned with.

A number of progressives indicated to me that they thought it would be useful for American officials to emphasize subtly to their Vatican contacts that we viewed the judicious use of birth control as an indispensable factor in the fight against underdevelopment. The Justice and Peace Commission stated to me on several occasions that they would welcome any subtle pressure we could marshal. Justice and Peace was convinced that there was a great urgency for an overhaul in Church doctrine on birth control. Father McCormack and Lady Jackson (Barbara Ward), both members of Justice and Peace, were leading critics of the official stand.

In February 1974, I arranged a private audience for a fascinating group from the Committee on Food and Population, which consisted of such luminaries as Dr. Norman Borlaug, the 1970 Nobel Peace laureate for his role in the Green Revolution. At the Vatican, they discussed "the implications of the world food situation, its relation to population and the importance of Vatican support for the actions proposed in the Declaration on Food and Population in this World Population Year." They planned to exert whatever pressure they could to assure that the Vatican attended the upcoming U.N. Population Conference in Bucharest. The Vatican did attend, but with a generally conservative delegation that ended up making no welcome departures on birth control but gratefully did not go overboard in pushing their traditional position.

During my five years in Rome, we maintained a continuous dialogue with the Vatican on many levels over matters of population. While the need to face the issue of birth control was always present, we did our best to weave it in more subtly in our general discussions on the question of the world's growing population. We provided the Vatican with considerable documentation on population matters and also arranged for impressively high-level visitors to discuss this issue with leaders in the Vatican, including the Pope. There always seemed to be a glimmer of hope for some at least moderate change in the Church's outright condemnation of all forms of artificial birth control, but nothing concrete ever really developed. The Vatican's expressed hope was always that economic and social development of the third world would lead to the practice of more responsible parenthood and thus a fall in birth rates. That was, of course, true, but the Vatican failed to see that the basis of that trend in the developed world was in fact the practice of artificial birth control. The Vatican simply refused to face the irrefutable fact that people in developed countries practiced birth control, irrespective of their religion— Catholics included.

XVIII

The War Against Drugs

Nothing could have been more of a natural for the Vatican than the war on drugs. It was a moral and health issue that contained no controversial aspects, as did the question of population and its spiny conundrum of artificial birth control. In spite of this fact, the Church had given surprisingly little attention to drug abuse and only on a few occasions had the Pope spoken out publicly on the matter. On his first visit to Rome in July 1970, Lodge came equipped to seek Vatican support for moving the French Government to do more to interdict clandestine drug shipments passing through their country, especially through the port of Marseilles. The Pope responded positively to Lodge's request and assuredly did raise the matter with the French, making clear that he felt strongly about this American initiative.

In October 1971, I arranged meetings at the Vatican for the State Department's Senior Narcotics Adviser, Nelson Gross. In addition to speaking with the Vatican's working level narcotics specialist, Fr. Jean-Pierre LeGall, he had a fruitful meeting with Archbishop Casaroli. Gross reported on the meetings he had with drug officials of the Italian Government. He noted that while he had a meeting of the minds with officials at the higher levels, he believed that the commitment to combat drug traffic had not filtered down sufficiently to the working level. He then asked if the Vatican could attempt to use its considerable moral force to move the Italians, as well as the Latin Americans, to greater responsiveness. Casaroli was particularly interested to learn of the situation in Italy, and he assured Gross that the Holy See would do everything possible to encourage foreign governments to vigorously attack the drug trade. In Latin America, Casaroli worried that many governments would give assurances and then fail to comply.

Casaroli noted that the Pope was deeply convinced of the drug problem's gravity, supported developing a world policy on narcotics, and was interested in keeping abreast of developments in the United Nations. Once the UN developed a firm stand, the Holy See could get behind it and give it a push. As an aside, Casaroli expressed the fear that in some countries, certain powerful and well-connected business interests may be involved in perpetuating the drug traffic.

An interesting insight into the success that our mission had in stimulating Vatican interest in the war on drugs came in a friendly conversation I had with a diplomat at the Yugoslav Embassy to the Holy See. He said that when President Tito and Pope Paul spoke privately in March 1971, they dwelt heavily on the problems of modern youth, with heavy emphasis on drug addiction. Following the audience, President Tito reported to his staff that he was quite surprised at the Pope's deep knowledge and keen interest in the subject. My impression was that the Pope's interest in these matters stemmed from our frequent interventions with him on the subject.

Our suggestions that the Pope make a major statement on drug issues bore fruit, but only after a long period of gestation. We had suggested a meeting of all Vatican figures interested in drug traffic, which eventually took place in June 1972. However, the Pope did not finally get around to issuing the long-awaited statement until December. Addressing a large group of Italians working on anti-drug campaigns in the schools, he stressed the importance of old-fashioned family values and the need for families to remain close to their children. He also called for a more sympathetic understanding on the part of parents for members of a younger generation that is often alienated from the older generation.

During my years in Rome, the Catholic Church in various countries did institute training programs on drug abuse for clergy and Catholic schoolteachers. These training programs, sometimes the result of prodding from the Vatican, helped to raise awareness of the problem. It was an important start and often was the first time that these people had really focused on drug abuse and learned anything concrete about its nature and the various means to combat it. Our mission could take some credit for getting this process underway.

The Pope greeting Robert Illing

XIX

Epilogue

In the end, what was the value of the Lodge Mission? Did it provide any truly useful benefits to the United States Government? Initially, our main concern was, understandably, the Vietnam War. In this regard, the Vatican proved a valuable asset in improving communications with our prisoners of war being held by the North Vietnamese. Also of great importance was the help that the Vatican gave at our behest to heighten awareness of the battle against drug traffic among leading figures in the French Government. Yet what unexpectedly turned out to be of inestimable value was the vast volume of information we gained from our myriad contacts within the Vatican bureaucracy. There was rarely a country, international problem, or incident in which the Vatican was not involved directly or at least indirectly, as our voluminous reporting over the five years I was there bears testimony. As a Muslim diplomatic once told Cabot Lodge when he was asked why his country maintained a substantial presence at the Vatican, "We don't want to miss anything."

The urbane and cosmopolitan Henry Cabot Lodge was clearly an excellent choice for establishing a serious relationship with the Holy See. The Pope and his collaborators saw in Lodge the best of America. With his flawless French, his enquiring mind, and his deep knowledge of history, Lodge fitted smoothly into the Vatican world. One of our best contacts in the Curia suggested to me early on that Lodge should begin to cultivate socially some of the top Vatican leaders. I passed this suggestion on to Lodge, who enthusiastically followed it. The same contact told me that the Pope probably got more from talking to Lodge than he did from most of his lay visitors.

Lodge was a man with incredibly broad contacts generated through over 50 years of working in international affairs, and the White House often asked him to hold conversations in Rome with a wide variety of important figures who were passing through. For example, in 1972, three years before the death of Franco, Lodge spoke at length at the Spanish Embassy to the Holy See to Crown Prince Juan Carlos. He also had discussions with King Constantine of Greece, who came to live in a lovely villa on the Appian Way shortly after the military coup that deposed him in 1974. At the end of his talk with the King, Lodge told him that he was sure that such an intelligent, attractive, and resourceful young man could easily make a success in another field as other former crowned heads had done. Constantine replied with great sadness that he didn't want to be a success in another field; he wanted to go back to being King of Greece!

Following his exile from Afghanistan, King Zahir Khan lived for some time in the Grand Hotel in Rome. As our offices at that time were in the hotel, I crossed paths with him frequently. Seemingly with time heavy on his hands, his Minister of the Royal Court Mr. Mohammed Ali used to sit for hours almost every day in the lobby of the hotel reading western cowboy stories in English. Maybe that was one of the problems with Afghanistan.

The five years I spent working with the Vatican were extremely satisfying, both on the professional and the personal level. The intellectual quality of the top Vatican officials was truly of a high order. Well-rounded and as a rule socially engaging, they invariably proved to be very good company. I spent numerous pleasant social moments in the company of my Vatican contacts, especially in one-on-one lunches at many of Rome's agreeable restaurants. Of course, it must be admitted that the caliber of people working at the top levels of an organization like the Holy See were not the typical clergyman that one might find at the local parish church. One could clearly say that only the best gravitated toward the top of such a worldwide organization. The exceptions, of course, were those few who had been promoted in order to be removed from a position where they had been either a failure or an embarrassment. It is common throughout history for countries to send abroad troublesome figures to get them out of the country, and even the United States occasionally does this as, for example, was the case when FDR sent Joseph Kennedy off as Ambassador to the Court of St. James.

I am firmly convinced that Washington was sufficiently impressed by the value of a mission at the Vatican that they continued it beyond Lodge's resignation and in 1984 took the definitive step of finally establishing full diplomatic relations. Needless to say, the fears of upsetting groups in the United States that felt diplomatic relations with the Holy See would infringe upon the American concept of separation of church and state did not manifest themselves.

My service in Rome convinced me that for the United States to send Catholics as ambassadors to the Vatican was generally not the best policy. Most nominally non-Catholic countries like Great Britain, Denmark, Finland, etc. invariably sent non-Catholic ambassadors, often with the deputy chief of mission being a Catholic. The idea was that a Catholic on the staff was valuable and useful in comprehending some of the arcane aspects of the Vatican world. In a way, for America to send a Catholic ambassador to the Vatican would risk creating the false impression that there is something religious in the nature of the relationship. To avoid giving such a false impression I have come to believe that it is more prudent to follow the British example and not send a Catholic ambassador to the Holy See.

Any diplomat worth his salt will amass a vast array of useful contacts during each tour. A wise foreign office will keep close tabs on the contacts of each of its diplomats with an eye to assigning an officer for a second tour when he is a senior officer to a place where his contacts from an earlier assignment may have risen to high office. Sadly, the United States, unlike most European countries, does not take advantage of this valuable diplomatic asset. As a small example, in my five years at the Holy See, I became acquainted with Cardinal Wojtyla, who later became Pope, two archbishops who were to become secretaries of state, and dozens of others who made cardinal, nuncio, and other high-ranking officers of the Church hierarchy. My experience was, of course, typical. Just imagine how beneficial it would have been for the United States to have me assigned back to the Vatican ten years later when I would have found myself on intimate terms with people from the Pope on down. Regrettably, this could never happen in the United States for other reasons beyond the control of the State Department's personnel system: choice ambassadorships like the Vatican are invariably given to inexperienced and unqualified political appointees.

As we enter a new millennium, at a moment when the relative power of the United States is being reassessed, it is well worth examining just what should be the nature of diplomacy in this new era. I would suggest that diplomacy should be the practice of furthering the interests of our country while trying to create a more peaceful, just, and harmonious world order. To achieve this, one must understand that diplomacy is a process of seeking mutually advantageous solutions to outstanding problems. To create the proper atmosphere for this, the concept of adversarial relations must be banished. Only a cooperative attitude is conducive to finding the kind of lasting solutions that all parties desire. The Treaties of Versailles following World War I are the type of punitive solutions that one should seek to avoid; they only lead to a desire for revenge from the losers, as was the case with Nazi Germany. In this age of globalization, future diplomats must be trained to take a broader world view in which they harmonize their country's national interests with the greater good of the wider world. In my career, I came to believe that the top levels of American foreign policy were all too often in the hands of lawyers, professionals who are trained to win for their clients without regard for their opponents. This adversarial approach has no proper place in the future. Although it may be too soon to judge, it seems that under President Obama, the United States is beginning to see the wisdom and the necessity of this approach.

My personal story is a cautionary tale of the Foreign Service. Getting assigned as Lodge's assistant was largely a fluke. I was available, of the right middle-grade rank, and spoke fluent Italian. Not much else. What was expected to be a routine political officer job quickly evolved into running almost year-round a very active mini-embassy in everything but name. On a daily basis, I dealt both professionally and socially with a level of counterparts worthy of an ambassador and with subject matter of the highest substantive level. Ambassador Lodge, who had years of professional experience as an American diplomat, wrote glowing and detailed reports on my performance. What was the result? Virtually nothing positive! After Rome, I went back to the State Department to do very interesting and agreeable jobs but none of them took proper advantage of the level of experience and competence I had acquired in Rome. Why? The system basically said to me, "Hey, pal, you've had five fabulous years in Rome; what more do you expect?" Not the best way to run a railroad, if you ask me—but of course no one did ask me.

Sadly, one could write a book about the shortcomings of the State Department's personnel system. The Foreign Service Act of 1980 stipulates that even political appointees must bring to the position certain recognizable and quantifiable qualities and skills like language skills, background knowledge, local experience, etc. To say the least, the White House, or the Senate that must confirm all ambassadorial appointments, gives not the slightest attention to these requirements in the majority of cases.

It was inevitable and right that the United States eventually opened a full embassy at the Holy See. It is ironic, however, that our ambassadors now have lower visibility at Vatican ceremonies than did Lodge, never serving there long enough to get to the front row. We now have five diplomats assigned to the Vatican Embassy, a residence, a chancery, gardens needing tending, secretaries, chauffeurs, and other staff. The cost is many, many times greater than the tiny cost of the Lodge-type mission and I seriously doubt if the reporting load is much different.

Index

Photographs are indicated by *ph* following the page number.